THE
SPORTSMAN'S
DINNER
BUSINESS

PAUL FLETCHER

THE COMPLETE GUIDE TO A PROFITABLE EVENING

How to Increase Earnings
from Your Sportsman's Dinner
and Send Yourself Laughing All the Way to the Bank

or

How to Make Your After Dinner Mint

Queen Anne Press

Queen Anne Press
is a division of
Lennard Associates Ltd
Mackerye End
Harpenden
Herts AL5 5DR

First published 1999

© Paul Fletcher 1999

ISBN 1 85291 608 7

The author and publishers wish to thank Mike Newlin of MBN Promotions for his support
in developing this project and for his help in compiling the Appendices.

Cover design by Paul Cooper in association with Atom Design Group
Editor: Michael Leitch
Printed and bound in Great Britain by
Butler & Tanner Ltd, Frome and London

Who invented Stand Up Bingo (or Ognib as it is often called)? How much did the first Manchester United autographed football raise when auctioned? When did comedians start to entertain at sporting dinners? Who was the first After Dinner Speaker?. Nobody knows, Sportsman's Dinners have simply evolved over the last 30 years or so.

They continue to provide the financial lifeblood for many smaller Clubs, and superb entertainment for larger Clubs. Almost always they show a profit and the better they are run the more money they make for the Clubs.

For the first time all the best ideas come together in a single book. The author, Paul Fletcher, has been involved in the business of Sportsman's Dinners for over 20 years. During his time as Commercial Manager at a non-league football club, and later in the same role at Huddersfield Town FC, he was responsible for organising many such Dinners. Over the last decade he has also established himself as one of the most sought-after Speakers on the circuit, reaching the equivalent of the FA Cup Final of Dinners in 1993 when invited to speak alongside Rory Bremner and Sir Bobby Charlton at the Professional Footballers' Annual Awards Dinner at the Grosvenor House Hotel, London, filmed live on Sky TV.

The book looks into every aspect of the Sportsman's Dinner and brings together a multitude of ideas to help any organisation to capitalise on revenue opportunities. Whether it is the first Dinner or 101st Dinner, the book stresses the importance of attention to detail, timing, organisation and careful planning.

Although the book is intended to be an instructional manual for Dinner organisers, it is also littered with numerous anecdotes from Paul Fletcher's experience of 'The Sportsman's Dinner Business'.

Paul Fletcher is from the world of football who started his career with his home club Bolton Wanderers in 1966 and went on to become one of the First Division's most expensive signings when transferred to Burnley in 1970. In 1974 he scored the 'Goal of the Decade' against Leeds United at Elland Road in a famous (4-1) Burnley win.

Following 5 years as Marketing Director for an International Photographic Company and a spell as Commercial Manager at the infamous Colne Dynamoes he became Chief Executive at The Alfred McAlpine Stadium in Huddersfield which was voted Building of the Year in 1995.

Paul Fletcher led the partnership between Kirklees Council, Huddersfield Town FC and Huddersfield Rugby League FC to build the Alfred McAlpine Stadium, which in its first year staged some major sporting finals, including rugby league World Cup and rugby union tour matches. In July 1995 REM, one of the largest Rock Bands in the World sold out the Stadium on two consecutive nights. In July 1996 concerts by The Eagles and Bryan Adams established the Huddersfield Stadium as an International Rock Venue.

September 1996 saw Paul Fletcher return home to Bolton Wanderers to become Chief Executive of the £35 million Reebok Stadium which is said to be one of the finest Stadium's in Europe. Part of a 200 acre, £200 million development. In April 1999 he took up a new position as Director of Commercial Affairs for the English National Stadium Development Company. A subsidiary of the Football Association, the company is set up to build the new Wembley Stadium, which hopes to stage World Cup 2006.

Paul Fletcher remains one of the most sought-after Speakers, both at Sporting and Business functions. He also regularly attends corporate events as a keynote speaker talking on Teamwork, Leadership and the Quest for Excellence. He lives in Newchurch Village in the sundrenched Rossendale Valley in the heart of Lancashire and is married with two children. Also he is an active member of the George Formby Appreciation Society.

CONTENTS

PREFACE   7
INTRODUCTION   9

PART ONE: PLANNING   **13**
1   THE CHECKLIST   15
2   THE BUDGET   18
3   THE VENUE   31

PART TWO: EXPENDITURE   **39**
4   THE MEAL   41
5   THE SPEAKERS   47
6   THE COMEDIAN   61
7   THE COMPERE   66
8   THE AGENT'S ROLE   77
9   THE TICKET   83
10   THE MENU   88

PART THREE: INCOME   **125**
11   THE RAFFLE   127
12   THE DRAW   133
13   STAND-UP BINGO   137
14   THE AUCTION   143
15   OTHER FUND-RAISERS   147
16   SPONSORSHIP   157

PART FOUR: THE BIG NIGHT   **171**
17   THE ROOM   173
18   THE RUNNING ORDER   180

PART FIVE: OTHER IDEAS   **205**
19   THE TOASTMASTER   207
20   THE STRIPPER   210
21   THE ALTERNATIVE THEME   212
22   THE TESTIMONIAL DINNER   219
23   THE SCHOOLS DINNER   223
24   ADDITIONAL ENTERTAINERS   229
25   WHAT ABOUT EQUALITY?   232
26   CORPORATE ENTERTAINMENT   235
27   THE DAY AFTER   242

PART SIX: APPENDICES   **245**
Appendix I: Competitions   247
Appendix II: Choosing an Agent   275
Appendix III: Speakers and Comperes   277

This book is dedicated to all the Speakers,
Comedians and Comperes on the circuit, who all
complain about stealing each other's material
but, deep down, love each other to bits.
And especially you, No1, for getting me
started in this wonderful industry. Thanks.

PREFACE

The Sportsman's Dinner business has evolved over the last 30 years to become a million-pound industry. Almost every night of the week, all over the country, hundreds of organisations stage functions either to fund-raise or to celebrate. It is the money raised from these events that keeps many smaller clubs in existence. Rumour has it that the very first Sportsman's Dinner was held at Everton Football Club some time in the early 1950s. The Speaker was Joe Mercer and his fee was an engraved pen-and-pencil set.

Our typical Sportsman's Dinner is a men-only evening, designed to raise valuable funds for the host club or organisation, and principally attended by its members. It is a recipe that has worked extremely well in the past. Times are changing fast, however, and mixed dinners are coming increasingly into play. For more on this topic, see the section 'What About Equality?'

The main concept of this book is to bring together a multitude of miscellaneous ideas, gathered from hundreds of functions the length and breadth of the country, and share them so that all organisations can profit from them.

It is very rare that a Sportsman's Dinner loses money. The majority of Dinners fall into three categories: the profitable, the very profitable and the very, very profitable. The only difference between these three categories is ... organisation.

This book shows you how to get the maximum benefit from a well-organised, enjoyable function. If you succeed, it will be much easier to sell tickets for the next dinner. One of the secrets of success in this business is not to do one thing brilliantly well ... it's to do one hundred things competently.

Although I write predominantly about Sportsman's Dinners, to clearly state my own non-sexist viewpoint I begin with an apology. All writers have to grapple with the issue of gender. I regret an easy answer does not exist as writers are continually confronted with the choice of writing he or she. Alternating between the two becomes awkward, so I have chosen to use the traditional he in the desire to make the book as reader-friendly as possible.

INTRODUCTION

I have never come across a book written specifically about Sportsman's Dinners. These Dinners have just evolved. As organisers of functions attend other functions, they pick up ideas and slowly enhance their own fund-raising efforts. But, as most organisations average only two or three functions a year, they rarely get the chance to perfect their own Dinner and maximise its vitally important fund-raising opportunities.

In fact, sometimes a strange anomaly occurs. The organiser is so relieved that all his guests are sat down eating, and his expensive, unreliable star/celebrity guest Speaker has turned up, that he slowly relaxes, gets sloshed and sees the rest of the night decline into a disorganised free-for-all. At this stage he does not mind, he is happy. Only when he wakes up the next day does he count the cost of his complacency.

During the course of reading this book you will come across £MTs (money making tips) and IOTs (important organisational tips), highlighted in bold type. Here is the first one and, believe me, it involves money.

£MT
If you (or your committee) are responsible for organising a Sportsman's Dinner, do not drink more than a couple of glasses of wine until the end of the evening has been announced. Once everyone is sat down to eat, you and your committee are the most important people in the room.

After the function is over, the Speakers paid and the money counted (and locked away in a safe place), feel free to get stoned out of your brains if you so wish.

Stories and Anecdotes

Throughout the book you will find anecdotes like the one below. These have been gathered from over 15 years of organising, speaking and attending a variety of Sportsman's Dinners up and down the country. Should you wish to skip these stories, you will not miss any of the important information and advice about organising a Sporting Dinner.

'As an example of how costly complacency can be, some years ago I was at a function where the great Nat Lofthouse, OBE, the Lion of Vienna, donated for auction a beautiful limited-edition watercolour painting of himself playing at Burnden Park, Bolton. Autographed on the night, it was a collector's piece. As expected, it raised over £650. Then the next auction item went under the hammer. It was the following day before the organiser realised that no-one had taken the trouble to find out the identity of the mystery bidder who was prepared to pay £650. At the end of the night he had vanished, and so had the painting! (To stop this happening, a simple £MT is suggested in the Auction section.)'

Secondary Spend

It is often said that we are ten years behind the Americans. In the marketing of sporting events we certainly are, but now many professional football, rugby, cricket and other clubs are becoming wise to something the Americans worked out years ago. This is the concept of 'Secondary Spend'. When British football clubs were only deriving income at the ground through money taken at the turnstile, the American football organisations were persuading their spectators to spend additional money (secondary spend) once they were through the turnstile. Hamburgers, Coca-Cola, hats, nuts, flags ... the list is endless. American football is intentionally organised into four quarters (as against two halves in soccer) to capitalise on television advertising and also specifically to feed and water more spectators over the three to four hours that an American football game lasts.

This book looks at various acceptable types of secondary spend, which should not be thought of in the same terms as 'ripping people off'. We are all familiar with the terrible rip-off feeling when a Compere announces, 'Let's all write our name on a twenty-pound note ....'

At every function, over 95 per cent of the guests have extra money in their pockets. The small percentage who genuinely do not have a penny to spend, once they have bought themselves a couple of pints and a ticket to the dinner, must not be made to feel embarrassed and allowed to drift off to the toilets once the raffle-ticket sellers come around.

The successful evening is when all guests feel they have had value for money. Yes, they may feel they have spent a little more than they had planned, but they only just missed out on some great raffle prizes; and the Speaker was superb; and that joke the Comedian told is one they will retell at work all week. If you can make them feel like that, they are certain to buy a ticket for the next function.

So let's get on with some ideas. The first one is a vital ingredient that every organiser feels he can do without – a checklist.

To make it simple, we have prepared a comprehensive checklist for you. There are some blank spaces at the bottom for you to put your own personal items. This simple piece of paper can be worth hundreds of pounds to you on the night, especially if somebody has forgotten to bring along the raffle tickets! So the first important organisational tip is:

IOT
Always use a checklist.

During the course of the book I refer to various people in anecdotes and examples. When I do not want to name the person, rather than refer to them as AN Other or Joe Bloggs, I affectionately call them 'Dougie Doings'.

Who is Dougie Doings?

This term originates from a wonderful story told by Joey Jones, the ex-Huddersfield, Liverpool and Wales football international. Apparently, the great Bob Paisley, manager at Liverpool when Joey played there, could never remember the names of opposing players. So, to get his point over in team talks, he always referred to an opposing player as 'Dougie Doings'.

'... Tommy [Tommy Smith], you pick up, er ... Dougie Doings if he comes down on the left flank. Joey, tuck in behind Tommy if ... Dougie Doings runs behind him. And Emlyn [Hughes], keep an eye on ... Dougie Doings if Joey goes wide ....'

The only time Bob Paisley altered this terminology was when Liverpool played in Europe. Then, irrespective of which country they were in, the opponent was referred to as 'Alberto Doings'!

Part One

PLANNING

'If you fail to plan ....
you plan to fail'

1
The Checklist

In fact, two checklists are recommended. They are:

Checklist A – for the run-up to the event
Checklist B – for recording ticket sales.

The example that follows is based on an average 10-week run into the function date (some organisations like 3 weeks, some like 3 months). After the event, remember to keep your checklist as this will be valuable for next year's function. It will be an even better point of reference if you note any problems and suggested improvements.

Refer to the Checklist regularly during the last two weeks running up to your function, and always keep a note of payments you receive for tickets.

In a perfect world you should collect all ticket monies before the event. This is not easy, but it is even harder to do after the function. Neither is it a good idea to receive monies on the night, when you have 101 other things on your mind. Also, be prepared for at least one table (10 people) not turning up on the night. By this time you will have had to commit yourself to a quantity of meals, and collecting money from such people after the event is difficult without making enemies.

IOT
Collect all ticket monies before the event.

CHECKLIST A			
JOB	WEEK	COMMENTS	DONE
Decide on a date	1		
Prepare a budget	1		
Book the venue	1		
Select menu/order wine	1		
Book Speakers (room required?)	1		
Book Compere (room required?)	1		
Book Comedian (room required?)	1		
Decide ticket price	1		
Look for Sponsor	1–2		
Have tickets printed	1		
Confirm in writing to Speakers	2		
Apply for late licence	2		
Sell tickets	3–10		
Invite VIP Guests	3		
Assemble raffle prizes	6–10		
Organise auction prizes	6–10		
Organise raffle sellers	6		
Bingo tickets/numbers	6		
Buy raffle tickets	6		
Print menu	6		
Brown envelopes for draw	8		
£5 notes for draw	9		
Phone entertainers (to double-check)	9		
Arrange photographer (press)	9		
Table plan – table numbers	10		
ON THE DAY			
Complete running order			
Seating plan – top table			
Money for Speakers/Comedian			
VIP Guest List/Room			
Additional fund-raisers?			
Money – bank or safe?			
DAY AFTER			
Write thank-you letter to Sponsors, Speakers, venue, etc			

CHECKLIST B

Ticket Sales

Name	Tel No	No of tickets	Running total	Amount Paid

2
The Budget

I have often wondered how many organisations prepare a detailed budget or try to project a potential profit before their event. Theoretically, it is a relatively simple calculation as there are probably only three primary considerations:

1 Numbers attending
2 Revenue from ticket sales and fund-raisers
3 Cost of entertainers, room hire and meal.

I have also wondered how it is that some organisations will announce a profit of a couple of hundred pounds at the end of an evening when, at a similar function, with the same numbers attending, another organisation will have made a couple of thousand pounds profit.

The reason can often be traced back to the very first dinner. By setting a ticket price too low (in an attempt to sell all the tickets), a standard is set and this makes it very difficult to raise the price significantly at subsequent functions.

In that case, what should be the ticket price at an organisation's first function? Using ballpark figures, based on a minimum attendance of 100 guests paying £25 per ticket, a simple calculation is therefore:

Income

Ticket revenue	100 x £25	£2500
Fund-raisers	100 x £10	£1000
		£3500

Expenditure

Meal costs	100 x £12	£1200
Entertainers	£1000	£1000
		£2200

Profit on the night   £1300

(VAT has not been considered in this calculation; see 'VAT Implications' later in this section.)

Obviously, a multitude of miscellaneous income or expenditure items could considerably increase or decrease the profit projection.

Based on the above figures, 100 ticket sales = £1300 total profit or £13 per head profit. From a base attendance figure of 100, every additional ticket sold provides a large increase in profit. This is because the only expenditure against further ticket revenue is the cost of the meal. The cost of the entertainers has already been paid for within the sale of the first 100 ticket sales. Therefore, as the entertainers will usually cost the same amount whether they perform in front of 100 or 500 guests, the profitability on ticket sales above 100 is greatly increased.

For example:

Ticket sales	100	150	200	250	300	350	etc
Total income (£)	3500	5250	7000	8750	10500	12250	
Total expenditure (£)	2200	2800	3400	4000	4600	5200	
Function profit (£)	1300	2450	3600	4750	5900	7050	
Profit per head (£)	13	16	18	19	19.50	20	

£MT
If you double the ticket sales (ie 100 to 200), you treble
the profit (£1300 to £3600).

Let us look at the same equation with ticket costs of a) £20 and b) £30.

a) Ticket sales @ £20	100	150	200	250	300	350	etc
Total income (£)	3000	4500	6000	7500	9000	10500	
Total expenditure (£)	2200	2800	3400	4000	4600	5200	
Function profit (£)	800	1700	2600	3500	4400	5300	
Profit per head (£)	8	11	13	14	14.50	15	

b) Ticket sales @ £30	100	150	200	250	300	350	etc
Total income (£)	4000	6000	8000	10000	12000	14000	
Total expenditure (£)	2200	2800	3400	4000	4600	5200	
Function profit (£)	1800	3200	4600	6000	7400	8800	
Profit per head (£)	18	21	23	24	24.50	25	

The example that follows shows a typical profit-and-loss account from a function in Yorkshire in 1998. The event was held at a 4-star hotel, featured a star celebrity Speaker and sold a capacity of 350 tickets @ £35 per ticket. The event was also sponsored by a local engineering company.

Profit on function: £10,565.

Analysis of a Typical Function (1998) – Attendance 350, Ticket price £35.00*

EXPENDITURE

Meal cost – £17.50	£6125	
Room cost	–	
Speaker 1	1000	
Speaker 2	450	
Comedian	250	
Compere	200	
Menu print	260	
Ticket print	90	
Raffle sellers	80	
Raffle tickets	20	
Top table drinks	55	
Sponsors drinks	80	
Microphone hire	25	
Hotel expenses	95	
Raffle prize	100	
Auction prize	25	
Misc 1	40	Commissionaires
Misc 2	30	Taxis
Total Expenditure	8925	

INCOME

Attendance x Ticket price	12250	
Sponsorship (profit only)	1000	
Menu advertising	320	
Raffle revenue @ £7.50 per head	2625	
Draw revenue @ £4.50 per head	1575	
Auction 1	600	
Auction 2	500	
Auction 3	175	
Auction 4	95	
Misc 1	250	Own wine
Misc 2	100	Sponsored ticket
Misc 3		
Misc 4		
Total Income	19490	

Less expenditure	8925
Total profit on event	10565

*VAT is not accounted for in this example.

Your Budget

EXPENDITURE

Meal cost		
Room cost		
Speaker 1		
Speaker 2		
Comedian		
Compere		
Menu print		
Ticket print		
Raffle sellers		
Raffle tickets		
Top table drinks		
Sponsors drinks		
Microphone hire		
Hotel expenses		
Raffle prize		
Auction prize		
Insurance		
Misc		
Total Expenditure		

INCOME

Attendance & Ticket price		
Sponsorship (profit only)		
Menu advertising		
Raffle revenue		
Draw revenue		
Auction 1		
Auction 2		
Auction 3		
Auction 4		
Misc 1		
Misc 2		
Misc 3		
Misc 4		
Total Income		

Less expenditure

Total profit on event

Summary

Without a doubt the quantity of tickets sold holds the key to profitability. If you budget to sell a minimum of 100 tickets and your projected income exceeds your expenditure, this makes your function profitable. From then on, additional ticket sales increase your profit.

£MT
Ticket sales = The best way to increase Profit.

VAT Implications

There is one golden rule about VAT. If in doubt, ring your local VAT office for advice or consult with your accountant.

Although it appears very straightforward, VAT can become extremely complex. That is, of course, unless you are not VAT-registered, in which case you simply pay all the bills including VAT and charge a gross price for tickets, all of which goes towards your profit.

On the other hand, if you are VAT-registered the same £25 ticket must include VAT, and so only £21.28 goes towards the net profit.

But what about the grey areas? Do raffle tickets include VAT? If someone bids £1000 for an auction prize, does this bid include VAT or is it a donation to the Club?

To give a clear picture, the following projections have been checked out with a VAT office and two accountants, but as legislation and VAT eligibility change regularly, check your potential liability with your local VAT office.

The following tables and summaries show how accounts could be prepared for both a VAT-registered organisation and a non-VAT organisation. The example is based on 200 guests paying £25 per ticket.

EXPENDITURE
Attendance 200, Ticket price £25.00

Item	Details	Cost for VAT-reg organisation	VAT reclaimable	Cost for Non-Vat organisation
Meal cost	£15 pp	3000.00	525.00	3525.00
Room cost		400.00	70.00	470.00
Speaker (VAT-registered)		1750.00	132.75	882.75
Speaker 2		400.00		400.00
Comedian		300.00		300.00
Compere		125.00		125.00
Menu printing		125.00	21.87	146.87
Ticket printing		80.00	14.00	94.00
Raffle tickets		8.00	1.40	9.40
Raffle sellers		60.00		60.00
Top table drinks		30.00	5.25	35.25
Sponsors drinks		60.00	10.50	70.50
Microphone hire		30.00	5.25	35.25
Hotel expenses		150.00	26.25	176.25
Raffle prizes		250.00	*(43.75)	293.75
Auction prizes		150.00	*(26.25)	176.25
Misc 1		200.00	*(35.00)	235.00
Total		6118.00	812.27	7035.27

* not reclaimable

INCOME

Item	Details	Revenue for VAT-reg organisation	VAT reclaimable	Revenue for Non-Vat organisation
Sale of tickets	£25.00 pp	4256.00	774.80	5000.00
Raffle	£6.00 pp	1200.00		1200.00
Draw	£5.00 pp	1000.00		1000.00
Auction 1		400.00		400.00
Auction 2		200.00		200.00
Auction 3		100.00		100.00
Auction 4		50.00		50.00
Menu advertising*		300.00	52.50	300.00
Sponsorship*		500.00	87.50	500.00
Misc 1	Donations	300.00		300.00
Misc 2				
Misc 3				
Misc 4				
Misc 5				
Total		8306.00	914.80	9050.00

* Both sold plus VAT.

Summaries

a) For VAT-registered organisations:

Gross income £9050.00; VAT payable £914.80	Net	£8165.20
Gross expenditure £7035.27; VAT claim £812.27	Net	£6118.00

Total profit	£2047.00

b) For non-VAT organisations:

Gross income	£9050.00
Gross expenditure	£7035.27

Total profit	£2014.73

This shows that a VAT-registered organisation makes a profit of £32.27 more than a non-VAT organisation.

VAT Rules in Detail

1   Ticket sales
If you are a VAT-registered company, ticket sales are inclusive of VAT (unless stated otherwise).

2   Raffles
Raffles are exempt of VAT, but if you purchase an item for your raffle (eg a colour TV) do not claim the VAT back on the purchase.

3   Draws
Draws are not affected by VAT, but do not claim any VAT back on prizes purchased.

4   Auctions
These are treated as a donation to the Club and are not subject to VAT. Once again, if you have purchased any items do not claim the VAT back.

5 **Menu advertising**
If you are a VAT-registered company, VAT will be included in the purchase price unless stated.

6 **Sponsorship**
Once again, it should be stated clearly whether or not the sponsorship costs are inclusive of VAT.

7 **Meal costs**
If you are VAT-registered, the cost of the meal (normally quoted inclusive of VAT) is reclaimable.

8 **Room hire costs**
This is both chargeable to VAT and reclaimable.

9 **Speakers (and entertainers)**
This cost is reclaimable if they are VAT-registered. Usually, VAT-registered Speakers and Entertainers will provide a formal VAT invoice.

10 **Menu printing**
VAT is reclaimable.

11 **Ticket printing**
VAT is reclaimable.

12 **Raffle sellers**
The wages paid are not subject to VAT, but the raffle sellers must be told that they are responsible for paying income tax if appropriate.

13 **Drinks bills**
VAT is reclaimable.

14 **Hotel expenses**
VAT should be reclaimable provided the event organiser is incurring the cost.

15   Raffle prizes
Do not reclaim VAT on these items.

16   Auction prizes
Do not reclaim VAT on these items.

*   Raffles are not subject to VAT, but if you buy a raffle prize do not claim the VAT back on the cost of purchase.

*   Draws and fund-raisers such as Stand-up Bingo and Auctions are also exempt from VAT, but again do not claim back VAT on any items purchased.

You must also consider, if you are VAT-registered, how you will bill your Sponsors or sponsored tables. Although business entertaining expenses are not reclaimable, the VAT on advertising is. But it must be shown to be a fair proportion of the sponsorship fee, otherwise the VAT inspectors will ask questions. For example, if a sponsored table for 10 people costs £500 (including VAT), and as part of the sponsorship package a full-page advertisement on the back of the programme is included, the 'true value' of the advertisement can be detailed on the invoice:

INVOICE (example):

Table sponsorship – £500.00

Includes:

Table for 10 people	297.88	
VAT on sponsorship	52.12	350.00
Advertising on menu	127.66	
VAT on advertising	22.34	150.00
Invoice total		500.00

The VAT on the advertising element is reclaimable, whereas the VAT on the entertaining is not.

For detailed guidelines, see VAT Notices 700/65 'Business Entertainment', 701/45/94 'Sport and Education' and 701/1/95 'Charities'. These are available via HM Custom and Excise offices.

IOT
If in doubt, check with your local VAT office. They will be
pleased to advise you.

Insurance

If you are organising an event, the chances are that insuring it is not high on your list of priorities, but it is certainly worth considering.

Q   What happens to you and your event if:

*   The venue becomes unavailable
*   The entertainment cannot make it at the last minute
*   The caterers do not show
*   You have spent time, effort and money organising such things as printing, advertising, security and everything else that goes with it. Then you have to cancel at the last minute.

A   You are going to wish you had insured the event!

Insurance is available to cover any size of event for cancellation or abandonment if the following happens:

*   The pre-booked act fails to appear because transport has broken down, a flight has been delayed, or they have been held up in traffic, taken ill or declared medically unfit, and there is no suitable replacement available.

* The booked outside caterers, Speakers, entertainment or music fails to appear.

* Failure of electricity, gas or water at the venue.

* Food poisoning, infection or closure of the venue.

* Severe weather conditions resulting in essential venue staff or security being unable to attend.

* Cancellation of the event due to:
  Death, injury or illness to any person in the organiser's party
  Severe weather conditions preventing the organiser's party from attending the event.

Do not dismiss the idea of insurance because you think it is expensive – you will be surprised at the low cost.

Should you be acting as the promoter of the event, it may also be worthwhile considering Public Liability insurance. Cover is quite inexpensive and can offer insurance up to £10,000,000 if required.

For information telephone Entertainments Agents Insurance Services: 01702 301103.

3
The Venue

If this is your first function, there are a few simple guidelines to follow when selecting your venue. The options on types of venue are quite limited: hotels, sports and leisure clubs, function rooms, pubs with function rooms, large companies (who advertise function rooms for hire), and churches (which also often have function rooms to hire). Apart from those standard venues there may be a marquee, stately home, airport or village hall in the area, but whatever the venue four key ingredients must be considered. They are:

1 **A large room**
2 **Catering facilities**
3 **Bar facilities**
4 **Car parking.**

For your first function it is a good idea to select a venue which has experience of catering for the numbers you are expecting.

IOT
Do not take any risks with your first dinner, or it may also
double up as your last.

A large room is obviously essential, and to make an event viable the minimum number of attendees should be around the 80 mark. When considering a room, you need to decide whether or not the seating layout should be based on individual tables of, say, 8, 10 or 12, or legs (sometimes called sprigs), ie long tables with two guests sitting directly opposite each other.

IOT
If you are considering selling sponsored tables, ensure the
seating layout plan has separate tables.
Companies prefer individual tables when sponsoring.

The ratio of space required when comparing individual tables against sprigs is approximately 3:4, ie a room large enough to seat 75 people at individual tables would seat 100 at long sprig tables.

Be careful, however, that the room is not too big. It does not follow that where you can sit a lot of people you can also sit a few. Atmosphere is important once the night is under way, and it is impossible to create an ambience when 100 people are seated in a room large enough for 500. If the room is too large for the number of tickets sold, do not be tempted to spread out the tables to make the room appear full. This often has the opposite effect. It is a far better solution to pack tables around the top table to create a friendly atmosphere.

'Sometimes the perfect room is not available. In 1992, I was guest Speaker at a golf club in Huddersfield and was amazed when I arrived to be told by the club president that the attendance would be around 105. I quickly counted the seats around the top table, which numbered 45. I was then informed that this was the club's seventh annual dinner and it had always worked very well as guests sat in different rooms. Apparently, there were also 25 seated on the balcony and 35 in the bar area with the remainder scattered around the rest of the clubhouse, all linked together by a PA system to hear the speeches. Unfortunately for me (and probably most other Speakers who visited this function), all the older members sat in the main room, with all the 'revellers' in the other rooms. Although some risqué football anecdotes only raised a titter amongst the old boys, thankfully I could hear plenty of laughter down the corridors from the younger, more relaxed members.'

Apart from being too large, rooms can also be too high. Atmosphere can be lost in a cathedral-type building, and it is very rare to find a memorable function in a large, high room.

Hotel Venues

If the venue you choose is a hotel, do not be scared to negotiate with the manager. For functions of 100 and above, he will have carefully counted his profits per head on the drinks he will sell to your guests. He will also make a good profit on the meal. The cost of the meal and drinks is normally higher in hotels than other venues as overhead costs are obviously higher, but there are some areas for negotiation.

*   Make sure the prices quoted by the hotel are inclusive of VAT in case your organisation cannot claim back the VAT. An unexpected 17.5 per cent increase in your venue costs can make a nasty hole in your profits if you are not expecting it.

*   Room hire. Usually a hotel will waive the room-hire charge for large functions like dinners where both food and drink are sold to guests.

*   Negotiate a favourable bedroom rate (should any of your guests wish to stay overnight).

*   Try to negotiate a 'free' hotel bedroom and breakfast for your Speakers if they request an overnight stay. The bigger the name of the celebrity, the better your chances of a free room.

*   Insist that your hotel venue provides a PA system. Some hotels hire one in; if so, make sure they pay, not you (any decent hotel should provide a PA as standard).

*   Ask for a raffle prize just before you confirm the booking. Do not settle for a bottle of Scotch; a meal for two in their best restaurant is the minimum.

*   Finally, once you have received the hotel's final quotation, which includes the cost of food, room hire, etc, just say 'What's the best price you can let me have, if I book with you now?' Then stay quiet. This should save you at least £25 and as much as £100. If you are not offered a reduction, explain that you have to look at another venue

before finally deciding. Say a friendly goodbye and leave. If the manager has not telephoned you in two or three hours, ring him and pay the full price. It was worth a try.

* Find out in advance who will be the manager of your function on the night. If something goes wrong, you do not want to be chasing around the kitchens looking for someone to put it right.

* Finally, ask the venue to sponsor a table; they can only say no. However, if they do say no, this may even persuade you to find a hotel that will sponsor a table.

£MT
Insist that the hotel provides, at the very least, a raffle prize. A meal for two is always a good prize.

Then your Compere can say: 'Our third raffle prize tonight is a meal for two at this lovely hotel .... Or £3 in cash.'

Reebok and McAlpine Stadiums
If you are looking to organise an event in the Huddersfield or Bolton area, I recommend that you look at either the Alfred McAlpine Stadium or Reebok Stadium. Both have superb banqueting facilities (I would say that as I helped to design them!) that can cater for events from 50 to 500. Both have resident caterers Ring & Brymer, part of the Gardner Merchant Group. For information at Huddersfield's McAlpine Stadium ring: 01484 484100, and for Bolton's Reebok Stadium ring: 01204 673730.

Final word
Selecting the ideal venue for Sportsman's Dinners is one of the most crucial elements in organising the event. Much depends on the quality of the venue, from the room itself through to the catering, bar facilities and staff. If you are in any doubt as to where you should be going, you can give John Smith's, the brewers, a call on 0345 202020 for some friendly, helpful information.

Posthouse

Over 300 reasons why your first meetings should be with us.

You're looking at four venues that can handle meetings and conferences for well over 300 people. Fully equipped, purpose-built rooms with all the support services you could hope for.

Let's meet without obligation. **Call 0345 383940** now.

Posthouse Birmingham City, Smallbrook, Queensway, Birmingham B6 4EW
Tel: 0121 643 8171 Fax: 0121 631 2528
Capacity: up to 630 - Includes:
Meeting and conference room facilities • Business support services • Accommodation • Dining and Entertainment
Banqueting capacity - 560

Posthouse Newcastle-upon-Tyne, New Bridge Street, Newcastle-upon-Tyne NE1 8BS
Tel: 0191 232 6191 Fax: 0191 261 8529
Capacity: up to 550 - Includes:
Meeting and conference room facilities • Business support services • Accommodation
Dining and Entertainment

Posthouse Nottingham City, St Jame's Street, Nottingham NG1 6BN
Tel: 01159 470 131 Fax: 01159 484 366
Capacity up to 600 - Includes:
The Academy Conference and Meeting Suites • Business support services • Accommodation • Dining and Entertainment
Banqueting capacity - 600

The Queen's Hotel, City Square, Leeds LS1 1PL
Tel: 0113 243 1323 Fax: 0113 242 5154
Capacity: up to 700 - Includes:
Meeting and conference room facilities • Business support services • Accommodation
Dining and Entertainment
Banqueting capacity - 500

A division
of Forte Hotels

Part Two

EXPENDITURE

'Keep track of your outgoings'

4
The Meal

Unless your guests are all vegetarians, the choice of menu will have little significance ... provided that the quality of the food is acceptable.

IOT
Do not forget to order two or three vegetarian dishes –
just in case.

People attending a Sporting Dinner have a basic standard of food they find acceptable. Most guests understand the difficulties of catering for 100, 200 and often 500 all at the same time. Here are some basic standards of food and service that you should insist on:

1   **Traditional**
    Choose familiar favourites. Do not risk fish, pork or garlic.

2   **Warm**
    If you are using outside caterers, insist that the plates are warmed before the meal is served on them.

3   **Sufficient**
    Ask your caterers to go round each table to ask if anyone would like any more.

4   **Service**
    Ask your caterers to serve the meal within a certain time frame. A rough guide is that a three-course meal with coffee should be served and cleared in one and a half hours.

5   Timing

If your caterers take too long, your function could finish too late, spoiling the evening. Give them a timetable to work to, but make sure your Compere starts on time.

If there is one standard menu which is easy to serve, cost-effective and liked by most people, it is:

Starter	Spring of Vegetable Soup
Main course	Roast Beef and Yorkshire Pudding,
	Roast and Boiled Potatoes, Carrots and Peas
Sweet	Apple Pie with Cream
Final course	Coffee and Mints.

You can of course always add cheese and biscuits, remembering the famous French chef Jean-Anthelme Brillat-Savarin who said, 'A meal without cheese is like a beautiful woman with only one eye.'

Although fish is not always popular, since the advent of BSE salmon steak is becoming more and more common. Running a close second is chicken as a main course. An acceptable option (but not liked by everyone) is lamb (often lamb can be fatty and not filling) or meat and potato pie (a cheaper option but very filling).

Some menu items to avoid for large functions are:

*   Consommé or a cold soup
*   Smoked mackerel as a starter
*   Prawn cocktail or salmon (unless price does not matter)
*   Salmon as a main course
*   Prunes
*   Any dish with garlic.

'I once attended a Sportsman's Dinner at a cricket club just outside Huddersfield along with Eric Jones (ex-CID and an excellent Speaker). We had been invited by Ced Beaumont, a Yorkshire comedian old in years but young in spirit, who always has a smile on his face. It did not take long for Eric and myself to spot that there did not seem to be some of the traditional things you associate with Sportsman's Dinners, things like food, and knives and top tables and things. Just about 90 chaps sat around waiting to be entertained. Ced then gave us our instructions:

"Now these lads have to b'entertained and raise a few quid f't cricket club. Once you've both finished go t'urt bar an' get th'selves a pie. They're only 80p and bloody lovely. Thanks for coming." '

Cook-chill Catering

Many larger organisations, such as hotel groups and conference venues, operate a cooking process of 'cook-chill' when large numbers are involved. This process allows food to be prepared, cooked, stored and reheated for service at any time within five days. In essence, a single central kitchen prepares the food, which is then rapidly chilled and can either be reheated in the main kitchen or a satellite kitchen close to the function room. There are many benefits to the system which include:

*   Increased overall quality management of food
*   Increased food safety procedures (required by law)
*   No variation in food quality
*   Increased speed of service
*   All food is served to the customer at the same temperature.

So, if your venue manager mentions that the food will be cooked using the latest cook-chill method, do not for one minute think it will lead to a loss in quality. The system is one of the most efficient and hygienic methods of food preparation available today.

'This is especially true when compared to a function I attended at a small football club in Cumbria. At about 10pm I was out in the car park, getting a breath of fresh air, when I came across the caterer loading all his cutlery and crockery in the back of a transit van. I complimented him on the quality of the meal, especially how tender the beef was, particularly so considering the cricket club did not appear to have any kitchens. His reply was not quite as tasty as the beef.

"We do most of the cooking in the large ladies' toilets. As this is an all-male event, they're not in use. To get the beef tender, I cook it at home, soak it in hot water for a couple of days before loading it on the van cold. Then it doesn't really need a lot of cooking. So we heat up the plates, cut the meat on to the hot plates, pour boiling gravy on top and by the time it gets to the punter the meat's just right."

Needless to say, that night was not one of my finest after-dinner performances. The old food-business joke fitted the moment perfectly: "Catering tonight by Sam and Ella".'

Plated Meals

If you choose a reasonable-quality hotel as the venue for your event, the caterers will normally provide a 'silver service' operation to serve your guests. This simply means that each component of the meal is waiter/waitress served individually to your guests. In a variation on silver service, the meat/fish is served, and then guests help themselves to the potatoes and vegetables, which are left in silver trays on the table. This second method is referred to as 'family service'.

'Plated meal service' is when the complete meal is served to your guests on a plate. This will provide a quicker and more cost-effective meal service for your guests. Plated meals are not usually a standard service at quality venues, and are either offered by the hotel as an option, or can be requested by an organiser. On occasions when time is of the essence, such as Award Presentation Dinners or functions involving two or more guest Speakers, plated meals are worth considering.

The labour costs to the hotel when operating this type of service are cut slightly, so do not be afraid to ask for a price reduction if you choose this method of service. The concept delivers the whole meal of meat, potatoes, vegetables and gravy, on a plate, directly to your guests.

It is a fast and efficient method and will suit the venue and most of your guests. The only drawback is the fact that everyone gets the same size of helping. Therefore those with large appetites, who would normally serve themselves a large helping, will lose out. It is therefore essential for the waiters/waitresses to go around the table asking if anyone would like more. On the positive side, everyone gets a warm meal without having to wait for potatoes and vegetables to arrive.

£MT
Ask for a reduction in price if the hotel suggests serving
plated meals.

IOT
If the hotel serves plated meals, insist that guests are
offered larger helpings if required.

Wine

Depending on the venue, consider purchasing your own wine from a local wholesaler (on a sale or return basis). Even if you have to pay corkage to the venue, it is possible to make anything from £1 to £5 profit per bottle, especially if you build into your sponsorship packages 'free' bottles of wine for your sponsored tables. It is a bit of a hassle, but if one committee member takes on this task it could add a few hundred pounds to the evening's profit.

At a more expensive dinner, for example where big items are going to be auctioned, it will be worthwhile putting at least some 'free' wine on the tables for all your guests. Try to get it sponsored, but if not cost it into your ticket price. Many people nowadays are used to drinking wine with an evening meal, and you do not want to look stingy if you are clearly expecting them to dig deep in their pockets when the auction comes round.

There's Always One!

Every dinner has one person who, irrespective of the quality of the meal, Speakers, Compere, wine, etc, will always feel he must complain. A few too many drinks are all he needs to make him determined to air his views.

IOT
If someone complains, do not argue, especially at the end
of a night when fuses are short.
The following action is recommended:

1 Listen to the complaint.

2 Answer as follows: 'Thank you for bringing that to my attention. I will look into what you have told me and if you will ring me tomorrow, I will tell you what action I have taken!' Then, turn around and walk away.

Very rarely will you get the call, but quietly look into the problem just in case he is right (or just in case he rings).

Summary

Someone once said, 'If the soup had been as warm as the white wine, and the wine as old as the fish, and the fish as young as the waitress and the waitress as willing as the barmaids, it would have been a very good meal.'

A good meal is expected. A bad meal can ruin your night.

5
The Speakers

After Dinner Speakers come in all shapes and sizes and from a variety of occupations. Around 70 per cent of Speakers attending Sportsman's Dinners are themselves from the world of sport. Predominantly they are from cricket, football, rugby league and rugby union, boxing, horse racing and snooker. Also well represented are Speakers who are ex-referees or umpires.

The other 30 per cent of After Dinner Speakers on the Sportsman's Dinner circuit are either from the world of entertainment or from business and industry. Entertainment is represented by actors, film and TV personalities, TV commentators and radio personalities. Business and industry Speakers are from a multitude of occupations: judges, solicitors, blacksmiths, bank managers, surgeons, steeplejacks, policemen ... the list goes on and on.

All the above have one principal virtue – either the ability to sell tickets or the ability to entertain. The market sets its own standards and it is open to anyone who wishes to try his luck.

It does not always follow that the International Sporting Celebrity, charging a large fee, will entertain your guests. But selling tickets is an easier job if your guests think your Celebrity Speaker will have some interesting and humorous stories from their times spent with household names and their memories of important matches. Equally, it can be much harder to sell tickets if your Speaker is a brilliantly funny orator, but does not have the 'orange box' of a well-known name to stand on.

It is not unknown for the 'Top Celebrity Star', with the wonderful TV image, to be a real pain when he attends a dinner. Stories abound of 'prima donnas' arriving late, leaving early and walking away with all the evening's profits as their fee. Yet some of the biggest celebrities and internationally known stars are most genuine and friendly and will make a real effort to ensure the evening runs smoothly. Chatting to the Chairman, signing autographs, acknowledging the sponsors and even giving back their fee for the evening, either to charity or as a contribution towards club funds. (Such celebrities are, however, few and far between.)

To avoid disappointment, you should state exactly what you require from your Speaker as part of the fee you pay. Often an agent will note these requests on a contract. But, just to be sure, if you want your Speaker to attend the dinner before he speaks, tell him (or his agent) that this is what you require. If you want him to stay until the end of the night, tell him this also. The Speaker then has a chance to consider your request before he accepts the booking.

In the unlikely event of something unexpected happening on the night, which requires him to arrive late or leave early, he will then need to contact you and ask your permission, or he risks breaking his verbal contract.

Another method of making sure the Speaker stays until the evening has officially ended is to state on the confirmation letter that '... you will be paid in cash (or cheque) at the end of the evening'. There can be no misunderstanding if this is stated.

Under normal circumstances, your Compere, Comedian and Speaker will be working as a team, all there to perform well individually, support each other and ensure the evening is a great success. Out of common courtesy, your entertainers should arrive on time and stay until the end – unless unforeseen circumstances prevent this.

Here are a few ways to help your Speakers, Comedian and Compere:

*   Send a map with a confirmation letter. This will help each of them to arrive on time.

*   Meet each one (or have someone meet him) at the front door of the venue. The bigger the name, the more people will want to speak with

him before he gets into the function room. Meeting him lets you know when he has arrived. If you do not do this, there is a risk that he will be 'ambushed' and taken to a private room for drinks and a chat with your guests without you knowing he has arrived.

*   Always seat your Speakers towards the centre of the top table – never at the ends and preferably next to someone who will act as his host.

*   Consider who you will seat next to your Speakers, and try to make it someone friendly or interesting.

*   Never video, photograph or record the speeches without the prior permission of your entertainers.

*   Never pay your Speakers by counting out cash on the top table. This can cause severe embarrassment.

*   Have the payments for your Speaker, Compere and Comedian ready beforehand, either a cheque or cash in a plain envelope. Discreetly pass this over at the end of the night, preferably in a quiet room away from proceedings.

*   Never disclose (especially to the audience) how much your entertainers are being paid.

*   After the event, always say goodnight and preferably walk with him to the door of his car.

*   If you want to make a real impression, send a simple postcard the next day either to the Speaker (or his agent), thanking him (provided, of course, he has performed and behaved to your satisfaction).

Every effort should be made to ensure your Speaker performs well. Dim the lights, close the door, quieten the noisy table, tell the bar staff to stop banging the glasses, turn up the microphone and close the bars if necessary.

It is said that a Speaker is 'only as good as his audience'. It is up to the organiser to give him all the support he needs. He will probably take the same script to two or three other dinners that week, but there is only one function at which you want him to bring the house down – and that is at your dinner.

'I once attended a function for a Rugby League club in the North of England where a strange event occurred. Halfway through the meal, one of the guests on a table near the front of the room began to sing. He had obviously had too much to drink and it was really funny ... for a time.

I remember vividly the song, it was 'The Wanderer'. His colleagues on the same table even helped him initially as he serenaded them with "I love to go a wandering along the mountain track ...." Unfortunately, he was still singing when the coffee arrived, as he was through the raffle and comfort break. By this time, believe me, it was not funny. Yet, incredibly, the Compere, seated at the end of the top table, then started to introduce me, leaving the audience to try and silence the singer. The next few moments went something like this:

"Our main Speaker this evening (Valderee, valderah) is from (Shut that stupid bugger up) the world of football (Valderah, ah ah ah ah ah ah ah – Come on lads, shut him up) he played for Burnley (along the mountain track, I love to go a ...) and England .... (Put a sock in it) .... Gentlemen, please welcome (along the mountain track)   Paul Fletcher ...."

He was still singing as I stood up. I had no choice. I simply said: "Thank you, Gentlemen, I'm delighted to be here (Valdereeee, valdereeeee) but I have only one thing to say before I start my speech. Either my singing friend leaves the room ... or I do."

I gave the microphone back to the foolish Compere and sat down.

For a Speaker, there is a golden rule. You can battle with a critic, a clown or a loudmouth, but never with a drunk. I was pleased when the audience applauded loudly as I sat down. They had had enough of this buffoon as well. He would have ruined the night for everyone. Even the Comedian, who might have taken him on, would eventually have been worn down.

Finally, four of his tablemates rocked the singer back on his chair and carried him out to the car park, with him still singing 'Valdereee, Valdereeeee'.

After that the night proceeded somewhat quietly at first, but ended up a great evening.

However, better organisation (or a competent professional Compere) could have prevented this potential disaster from developing in the first place.

Footnote. At about 11.45pm, I was making my way back to my car when I noticed our friend the singer, flat out, snoring away in a drunken haze in the front seat of the car next to mine. I know it sounds cruel but it was a wonderful feeling as I slapped both hands on the side of the window, making an enormous bang. He must have thought a bomb had hit the car as he shot up, bolt upright, with his hair standing on end.

"Goodnight," I shouted. As I drove past him, he held his head in his hands. "I love to go a wandering, along the mountain track, I love to go ...." I sang it to him at the top of my voice as I drove out of the car park with the window down.'

The Driver

Many Comedians and Speakers like to be driven to an event. This allows them to arrive at a function fresh and relaxed, and have a drink afterwards. A drive to a function can be very stressful, especially for entertainers who like to arrive on time. However experienced you are, it is still an awful feeling to join the M6 on your way to Birmingham and find yourself caught up in a line of traffic as far as the eye can see. Is it roadworks or an accident? If it is roadworks you could be delayed for an hour, and if it is an accident it could be four hours or more.

Having a driver is no guarantee against traffic jams, of course, but at least the Speaker is spared the pain of actually driving through the crawl. The advent of the mobile phone or car phone has helped to relieve the tension. But arriving at 9.30pm and speaking at 9.45pm does not enhance any entertainer's performance.

At most functions the entertainer's driver will be provided with a meal (usually free of charge) and seated somewhere in the body of the function. There is always at least one spare seat because somebody has not turned up. It is customary to accept the Celebrity Speaker's driver at a table as a matter of courtesy.

It is never a good idea to sit a driver on the top table. This should always be reserved for VIPs. Even if every seat is taken, it is always possible to squeeze an extra seat in somewhere.

IOT
If you are unsure whether your Speaker will bring a
driver, leave a spare seat just in case (and make sure it is
not on the top table).

The Truth Room

The story goes that a Speaker or Comedian wanting to know how well he has performed will go to the toilet and lock himself in a cubicle. From there he will hear a true reflection of his performance from the guests queueing to use the toilets.

The toilet is therefore referred to as the 'Truth Room', and if you are an organiser and you are looking for a candid opinion of your event, Speakers, food, fund-raisers, etc, that is the place to go and listen.

Amateur Speakers

There is, of course, the Amateur Speaker to consider. This Speaker usually wishes to be informative rather than humorous. He may be a company chairman or director, a charity recipient, an industry leader, a politician, the winner of an award, a new club manager, captain, owner, etc.

Guests will often listen to this type of speech with great interest and not be looking to fall off their chairs with laughter. An 'informative Speaker' can offer an excellent way to start the evening's proceedings.

He may build into his speech a humorous anecdote or joke, which will usually be received with courtesy at the start of a function. The same story, told at the end of a great night, could well nosedive.

IOT
Unless there are very special reasons, or the speech will
only last a few minutes, never introduce an amateur
Speaker after your professional entertainers.

Then there is the Amateur Humorous Speaker, with whom there are no grey areas. They are either very good or disastrous. We have all been at functions where the unskilled but well-prepared Chairman gets to his feet with a ream of A4 typewritten notes in his trembling hands. Once his first joke is greeted with silence, he starts to panic as he knows he has another 10 jokes following which are not as good as the first one. But he continues on and on, deeper and deeper, longer and longer, while embarrassment and an undercurrent of chatter creep into the room.

Fifty minutes later, he sits down in a lather of sweat, knowing the applause is really because he has finally sat down.

'In 1994, I was invited to speak at a golf club in Lancashire that will remain nameless. On arrival I wandered round the Club for ten minutes and finally found the Captain and his committee very well oiled at around 7.45pm. As I stood at the edge of the conversation, it was quite obvious that this was going to be their night. An evening for them to wallow in their own self-importance.

It reminded me of a wonderful line the Preston comedian Wandering Walter used to use:

"You meet some lovely people at golf clubs, and you also meet some ****s." This Club had more than its share of the latter.

We finally marched in at about 9pm (I marched, the Captain staggered) and on the top table sat 19 of the good and godly. The Captain sat directly in the centre with the full regalia – carved chair, ex-Masonic lodge; engraved gavel (which read "I was right. Wandering Walter"); radio microphone, as he was also Compere; a top-table lectern holding his notes (you are right, a ream of A4 paper), a bottle of Scotch and one crystal glass.

I sat quietly in the next seat to the end, alongside the deputy greenkeeper. The Captain Elect, who was to be the second Speaker after the Captain (I was third) sat on my right.

Within the hour, a few tell-tale signs told me this would not be a normal night. Little things like a public telephone directly behind the top table that was receiving regular incoming calls. Probably half the audience of 90 guests used this as the evening proceeded.

The microphone, which was being installed and tested by the Steward as we had soup, was directly from a Norman Collier sketch, but the Captain was not concerned that his guest could only hear every other word he said. He was not really bothered. The whisky bottle was almost empty and his committee was sucking up to his every (other) word.

To my right, the Captain Elect started to interest me. This was quite pleasing as the deputy greenkeeper on my left had gone into a drunken sleep, head on hands, on the table – to the amusement of Table 1 who poured gravy and salt into his hair. "That'll teach him to **** up the 6th green!" they said as they tied his shoelaces together and ate his pudding.

The Captain Elect was very, very nervous and asked me if I would read, and comment on, his speech whilst he got himself (and the Captain) another Scotch. I obliged as I sipped my orange juice (I was driving home).

His speech had been partly written and typed by his secretary who had "found him some jokes to tell". She had highlighted the "really, really funny" jokes in luminous red (four of them) and the other twelve jokes in colours of lesser hilarity. This was done, he said, so that he would know how long to let the audience laugh before going on to the next anecdote.

He returned with a large Bells and asked, "What do you think?" I knew his speech had disaster written all over it – unless he could deliver it in such a way that the audience would find his jokes so bad, they would laugh at him rather than with him.

I replied in the only way that I could. "It's too late to change anything now. Don't have anything more to drink and deliver it as best you can, and always remember to smile."

His reply was, "Keep an eye on my notes, I need another drink!"

At this stage a dignitary from the top table went completely white and it was thought he was having a heart attack. The Club Secretary queued for the phone and rang for an ambulance. The old boy was carried to the back of the room and laid out on the pool table to await the ambulance ... whilst the speeches began. Nothing was going to spoil the Captain's big night.

To cut a long, sad story short, at around midnight the Captain Elect was asked to speak and I helped him to his feet. Meanwhile, three para-medics administered life-saving techniques as they carried the dignitary from the pool table to the ambulance. I have no doubt I was the only sober person in the room. Without exception, the others were either drunk, asleep, fighting outside or being ill in the toilets (or dying on the way to hospital).

The Captain Elect began but, before he could say a word, someone in the room shouted "Sit down, you drunken bastard." To which he replied with a similar vulgar comment and managed to drop all his notes on the floor.

His next problem was that he picked up his notes in the wrong order. If the audience had been sober enough to listen, they would have heard the funniest After Dinner Speech in the history of the club. After complimenting the ladies' section, he started to tell an old porky about an Englishman, an Irishman and a Scotsman in Germany in the war (marked in red). The story ended up as three nuns in a brothel in Turkey (marked yellow). I was absolutely howling with laughter, with tears rolling down my face when he collapsed and fell backwards unconscious to an enormous roar.

Three people who were waiting to use the telephone dragged him into the ladies' toilets adjacent to the top table, and I could see him laid out in there, flat on his back and snoring, all through my short speech. Needless to say, it was not my best performance ... as it is often difficult to get people to laugh when they are all drunk or asleep!

Footnote. During his speech the Captain commented on how disappointed he was in the drop in junior membership at the Club. I wrote to him the following week with a few suggestions as to why this might be happening. I was paid by cheque four weeks later. It was £10 short. I wrote back, insisting on receiving the full payment on principle. When I received it five weeks later, I sent it off to my favourite charity. Wandering Walter had been exactly right.'

So You Want to Be a Speaker?

At most libraries there are a dozen or so books telling you how to be a Public Speaker. They all give sound advice on how to research your audience; how to breathe from your stomach not your chest; how you only need a good start, a good middle and a good ending ... but they do not tell you where to practise. Sorry, but in front of the mirror does not work.

Most people who buy these books, I imagine, need guidance for one special speech. They are either a best man, a club captain, a bridegroom or a new chairman. For most people, the opportunity to stand up and speak does not come along very often. Because of this, very few people get the opportunity to become accomplished. However, I do not believe you can learn to be a Speaker by reading books on the subject. Speaking is like swimming, the only place you learn is in the water. You cannot learn how to swim out of a book, and it is the same with public speaking.

'I am often asked, "How did you become an After Dinner Speaker?" For most Speakers, I think the answer is the same: "By accident." Although I was always the joker in the pack during my time in professional football, I never considered standing in front of an audience and telling a few stories. In fact, much the opposite, I would avoid any opportunity of saying a few words into the microphone, even in front of the Under-10s football team! Playing in front of a 40,000 crowd was straightforward ... but speaking into a microphone in front of 20 kids and their mums and dads caused a panic attack. The fear of speaking (or the fear of looking a fool because you are tongue-tied) is a very real fear for many people. And I was no different.

Two things happened in the early 1980s which put me on the road to a regular spot on the top table. First came a Dale Carnegie course. After football I searched for ways to earn an honest living. I had read Carnegie's book "How To Win Friends And Influence People", and it had made an impression. So I enrolled on a once-a-week, 14-week evening course, not knowing quite what to expect.

I vividly remember the first night. I sat in a room with forty strangers and the instructor said, "I want everyone to stand up, tell me your name, where you live, and why you are here." I was at about number 35, and as it slowly got to my turn my heart was thumping at 250 beats a second. I was petrified. Had I not been in plaster up to my thigh as a result of a broken leg, I would have been out of the room and in my car long before my turn arrived to address this daunting group of strangers. But we were all in the same boat. And we all got through it.

Five weeks later, something happened that simply changed my whole outlook on life. I can still see the black felt-tip pen drawing a circle on a large sheet of paper and instructor Brendan Fitzmaurice writing the letters "CZ" in the middle. He went on to describe the Comfort Zone. He was talking about me. For sixteen years I had been wrapped in cotton wool, never needing to venture outside my Comfort Zone. Then Brendan Fitzmaurice said, "Where do life's opportunities lie, inside or outside your own comfort zone?" On the way home I decided I would never again shy away from a challenge because I was afraid of embarrassment, and to this day, over twenty years later, I do not think I ever have.

At about the same time my good friend Mike "No 1" King, the Comedian I mention many times in this book, rang me to ask if I would judge the "Miss Smith and Nephew Beauty Competition". Mike worked as PR Officer for the Smith and Nephew group of textile mills in East Lancashire, and as part of his job organised the annual beauty contest for the staff.

As the evening came to a close, the winner crowned and everyone ready to go home, Mike invited me up on stage in front of an audience of around 200. He asked me to say a few words. I was glad to, I was spending some time outside my comfort zone. I told a few stories about my time at Burnley, had a dig at Chairman Bob Lord, said goodnight and went home. Three days later someone from the audience asked me and Mike King to speak at their Sportsman's Dinner. We both said yes. It was our first dinner ... and someone in that audience saw us and asked us to speak at "their" dinner ... and that is how No 1 King and I got started.

I do not ever remember asking for a fee, or being paid a fee, for at least 12 months, but it did not matter, I was learning a trade. Listening to different Comedians, learning about timing, finding out what to do when the microphone breaks down, etc, etc. I was pleased to serve my apprenticeship.

In 1995 I was delighted to speak at the Professional Footballers' Annual Awards Dinner at the Grosvenor House Hotel, London, in front of 1250 dinner-suited footballers and their guests. Without doubt it is the FA Cup Final of after-dinner speaking. Forty-six people sat on the top table. I had Eusebio to my left and Sir Bobby Charlton (first Speaker) to my right. In fact, I was the only member of the top table I hadn't heard of!

My speech was well received. I had done my apprenticeship well. Someone asked me before I spoke if I was nervous. I replied, "Not half as nervous as I was some years ago in Bolton when I had to stand up and tell 40 people my name and address!" '

For information on Dale Carnegie courses ring 0161 766 3343.

The Captain's Speech

In 1994 Peter May wrote a superb piece about Sportsman's Dinners in FC magazine. He included in the article a DIY Awards Night speech that any Sunday footballer can use. It can of course be rewritten for other sports or occasions.

'Hello, my name is .... and I'm your host for the evening. We might be running a bit late tonight, but certainly not as late as one of ....'s tackles. Still, at least it's the first time that .... has ever been changed before the kick-off.

First, I'd like to thank ...., our sponsors, for their support, as well as our kit-washer ...., the ever-tireless club secretary ...., and all the wives and girlfriends present, who've put up with being football widows every Sunday morning.

Throughout this season we've continued to set standards – although, regrettably, most of them have been rather low standards where .... is concerned.

It's been a good/bad/atrocious/indifferent season [delete where applicable], but throughout this year of promotion/relegation/transition, all 11 players on the pitch – or, in the unfortunate case of the match against ...., all nine players – have given their all. Of course, we have lost some matches we shouldn't have. Next season we had hoped to have a dog as our mascot, but Battersea Dogs' Home was worried we'd lose the lead. Still, when we've been behind on windy January mornings the players have dug deep; in fact .... dug so deep, he almost bought a round. Almost, but not quite.

Our campaign has been built on clean sheets, something our keeper .... specialises in, although that's enough about his love life. Seriously, though, he's had a great season and has deservedly been described as the Stevie Wonder of the .... League.

Now, here's the moment you've been waiting for. We do have a mounted left leg that was separated from an opposition player by our team physio ...., and which is being presented later. But first I have in my envelope the names of the Players of the Year. Even that notorious gambler .... has closed his book on this one. It's a man who's shown more consistency than a pot of Dulux. Ladies and Gentlemen, ...

Thank you, thank you, but please settle down, because we have another trophy: the .... [city/town/county] Golden Boot, for our top scorer. When he came to this club it was said of him that if Jesus himself laid on the cross he'd miss the header. But this season he's been a revelation, shooting with the power of a rocket – and sometimes the same trajectory. Ladies and Gentlemen, the Robbie Fowler of .... is .... [announce any other award winners].

Thanks to you all for turning out this season; it's a squad game, and everyone has played their part, even ...., who managed to shrink the kits and dye them bright red/green/orange [delete as applicable]. And now it's the part of the evening you've all been waiting for – the free beer. Which means that even .... might be spotted at the bar. Thank you, and have a good night.'

Watch out for the Wardrobe!

No two functions are the same, and a Speaker has to learn how to cope with all eventualities. The strangest things can happen on the top table.

My good friend and speaking partner on many occasions, Fred Eyre, football's favourite failure and one of the most experienced and sought-after Speakers on the circuit, once addressed an audience of 3500 people at The Cardiff International Conference Centre (more than ever watched him play) and as few as ten for The Ford Motor Company in Yorkshire ... he's given bigger team talks!

Fred is now a media celebrity as well as the best selling author of fine books (remember 'Kicked into Touch'?). Here he recalls a particular function that was memorable for all the wrong reasons.

'It had developed into a super evening, the audience was wonderful to me – warm and spontaneous – and life was grand as I approached the middle of my speech. From the darkness, I became faintly aware of a little bit of movement, but nothing to cause any problems, I thought, until I picked him out like a moth in the spotlight, a big, plump-looking geezer with a bald head.

I still did not pay much attention to him, and the audience was still laughing loudly at my last line when he lurched out from behind his table and came swaying towards me like an MFI wardrobe.

Sometimes, in situations like this, I may make some reference to a person wandering about: "Is it a sponsored walk or can we all join in?" or "OK, sit down now, we've all seen the suit!" But this was such a high-class event that I simply decided to ignore him and allow him to go to the toilet in peace.

A few strides later and he was standing slap-bang in front of me. I noticed a bulge under his jacket, but did not give it a thought until he unbuttoned it and produced a soda siphon, full to the very top, and proceeded to hose me down with it from head to foot, until every last drop had gone from the bottle. I'd finally reached saturation point!'

That evening was definitely the highlight of Fred Eyre's career as an 'extinguished' After Dinner Speaker.

6
The Comedian

What better way to round off a great night than listening to a very funny Comedian. Incredibly, no matter how hard you try, you just cannot remember the jokes to tell your friends and workmates the next day. Even if you can, retelling the story in the cold light of day does not make it quite as funny as it sounded the night before. Was it the atmosphere, or the wine, or the contented feeling after a good meal, or is it the 'way you tell 'em'?

A Comedian can also ruin a function. He can be too blue, or too mild, or too cocky or too relaxed, or he can simply have a bad night and 'die on stage', as they say.

It is said that there are only four or five jokes. Every humorous story is based on a set situation. That only leaves the interpretation or the telling of the story. In fact, jokes do not have to be new to be funny. My old friend Mike King, often regarded as one of the best Comedians in the country (by himself), has been telling one particular story for about twenty years that I know of – even to the point where this joke gets 'requested' by the audience. How often have I heard Mike asked, 'Tell us the one about the fruitcake.' I must have heard the joke over a thousand times, yet still laugh my pants off when the fruitcake comes into the story. It is a great joke which, like a good wine, matures with age.

Bad Language

Bad language, swearwords or obscenities do not often offend women, but may be extremely embarrassing to the men who are in their company. Some Comedians have made a name for themselves based on vulgarity and crudeness, but few are seen on the top table at a Sporting Dinner – Praise the Lord!

'In 1992 I was invited to speak at the Gary Bennett Testimonial Dinner in Sunderland. Gary had been awarded a testimonial year by Sunderland Football Club and the dinner was one of a number of fund-raising events organised by his committee.

The Comedian that evening was Roger De Courcey of "Nookie Bear" fame, who I had not met before. Roger was seated a few places from me on the top table and I did not have much opportunity to speak with him until about 9.30 in the evening.

The event was held in a large, sports hall-type room, and was packed to capacity with around 400 or so guests who included Sunderland players, their wives and Gary's friends and family. Obviously it was a night to be clean and courteous.

When I finally got chatting to Roger, I was quite unaware of his after-dinner act. Although I had seen Roger occasionally on the box, I had never worked with a ventriloquist at a sporting function. Before the dinner, I had seen Roger position Nookie Bear, in his box, directly behind himself on centre stage.

As we chatted for the first time, I happened to comment that there were a number of women in the room, and a lot of Gary's family and friends were sitting immediately in front of the top table. I said to Roger, "Do you swear in front of an audience like this?" "Under no circumstances!" came Roger's curt reply. I was quite taken aback by his abrasive tone.

He then added, "But unfortunately the bear swears his ****ing head off." I laughed at the remark and made my way back to my seat, not knowing quite what to expect.

My speech was well received by a largely football audience. It was enjoyable to reminisce about playing at Roker Park and other magnificent North-East clubs, like Hartlepool United (are there any other teams up there?).

Then Roger De Courcey was introduced. After a few warm-up jokes he opened the box and brought out Nookie Bear. I will never forget Nookie's opening lines. They went like this:

Roger: "Good evening, Nookie."

Nookie: "Evening. Where are we tonight then?"

Roger: "We're up in Sunderland at the Gary Bennett Testimonial Dinner."

(Pause while Nookie sighs)

Nookie: "Gary Bennett? I've never ****ing heard of him."

The audience, me included, nearly fell off our chairs with laughter, especially the players' table and Gary's family.

(Nookie then swivels his head to weigh up the top table)

Nookie: "Roger, is Gary Bennett the ugly ******* sat in the middle?"

The room erupted. The next thirty minutes were electric as this inoffensive little bear ripped into everyone he (or Roger) could think of. Nookie's language was appalling and wonderful, both at the same time.

Had the story about Nookie's encounter with a duck been told by Roger himself, it would not have gone down well in front of a mixed audience. But Nookie somehow got away with it. Since that date I have had the pleasure of working with Roger De Courcey and Nookie on a number of occasions and can only describe the act as simply magnificent.

I wish I had the space to relate the evening at Huddersfield Town when Nookie laid into the then Chairman of Huddersfield Town, Geoff Headey, a wealthy local businessman who imports wickerware.

"... I've spent 13 hours in the boot of a car, squashed up in a wooden box, and the minute I'm let out who am I sat next to .... a ****ing basket maker!" '

Offensive Racist Remarks

Offensive racist remarks, or offensive racist jokes, are thankfully no longer acceptable at most sporting functions. In fact, in recent years I have heard offensive racist jokes greeted with silence as audiences let Comedians know that in these times such stories are inappropriate.

But every country has its funny idiosyncrasy or accent and a humorous, inoffensive joke always gets a good reception irrespective of the accent. Jokes are told about every nationality, mostly the Irish, but funny stories abound about the Scottish (being tight), Australians (being rude), Americans (being boastful), Germans (putting towels on deck chairs), Welsh (normally about sheep or singing), Indians and Pakistanis (either cricket or corner shops), the list goes on and on. If the accent is realistic and the storyline does not offend, it is sure to get a laugh.

'I like to think that my good friend Mike No 1 King has perfected the Indian/Pakistani joke without being offensive. For many years Mike worked as personnel manager for a group of mills in East Lancashire and developed a magnificent relationship with a large Asian workforce, talking to many of the workers "in their own accents".

I once attended a dinner with Mike at a Working Men's Club in West Yorkshire, just outside Bradford. It was a true multicultural event with representatives from the Caribbean countries and Asia. Mike was on his feet for 45 minutes and told humorous stories in a range of accents including German, Australian, Pakistani and West Indian. Just as we where leaving the venue around midnight, we were met in the foyer by a group of ten, all of Pakistani origin, who had sat together on a table in the middle of the room. I was wondering if they had taken offence when their spokesman said, "Mr King, we enjoyed your act so much we want to book you for our event in May. We have our own cricket club and have been trying hard to get a Pakistani player to attend our function but can't. You're the next best thing as you sound just like my Grandad who lives in Islamabad!"

I did not attend the function but I believe Mike was again superb (so he said) in front of a 90 per cent Asian audience. Integration indeed.'

Choosing a Comedian

A good professional Comedian will be able to assess his audience and perform in line with the requirements of the night. At one end of the spectrum is the formal black-tie dinner of the DD Veterans Society and wives, who require a witty performance without any swearing or crudity. At the other end is the DD Annual Rugby Union dinner, where they will be looking for a Chubby Brown-type of 'anything-goes stag performance'.

Most Sporting Dinners come somewhere in the middle of the spectrum. By booking through an agent (and there are some agents who only handle Comedians), you can discuss your requirements to ensure you get the type of Comedian you are looking for.

Alternatively, you can book a Comedian you have heard previously at another function, or even book a Comedian on a recommendation from a friend, but it is always a good tip to ask for a second opinion.

If the budget allows, there are also a few affordable 'big names' from TV. They will certainly sell the tickets and provide glamour, as well as humour, to the evening.

Mixed Roles

Some Speakers are specifically booked instead of a Comedian to round off the evening by making the audience laugh. These Speakers usually include an element of joke-telling in their act (to the annoyance of most Comedians) and often require a far larger fee than a Comedian would ask. Something, however, is missing, certainly on the value-for-money front. It can be the same joke, told with the same delivery and the same accent, and get the same amount of laughter, but if it is told by a Speaker (who may be a footballer, bank manager or judge), minute for minute it will cost over twice as much as if it were told by a Comedian.

Sometimes a Comedian will double up as a Compere (to the annoyance of Comperes). Many Comedians find it easy to 'top and tail' the night with an introduction, then raffles and auctions followed by a 30-minute 'spot'. They will do this for a small extra fee, normally equivalent to 30 per cent of what would be paid to a 'professional' Compere.

7
The Compere

A good Compere is a great investment. Many organisations see the role as an opportunity to save money by getting somebody they 'think can do the job' to be Compere. This somebody can be anyone – the chairman, a local celebrity, the club captain, a local character, a team member known for being the joker in the pack, a newspaper sportswriter or even the event organiser himself. In doing so, they are taking quite a risk. Probably the amateur Compere will have little concept of the role, and at best his experience will be limited to a couple of previous efforts; almost certainly, the job is not one he does on a regular basis.

A good experienced Compere has four functions. If he performs these well, he pays for himself. They are:

1   **Start and finish the evening on time**
2   **Introduce (correctly) the guests, guest Speakers and Comedian**
3   **Announce other items (raffles, toasts, etc)**
4   **Capitalise on all fund-raising opportunities.**

An auction is an excellent example of how a good Compere will earn his salt. Experience will tell him roughly how much a certain item will raise at each function. Most Speakers will tell you how they have seen a Manchester United Autographed Football (one of the commonest auction items) be sold for £25 (by a bad auctioneer or Compere) or up to and over £1000 by a good Compere.

Like a good referee at a football or rugby match, a good Compere (unless he is also able to be funny) will hardly be noticed during the course of the evening. He will intentionally play second fiddle to the main entertainers. He will also know exactly when and how to introduce the main Speakers and Comedian.

To summarise, do not underestimate the importance of the Compere. A Compere should be seen not as a cost item but as someone who can increase your organisation's income.

The Welcome

If a professional Compere is not employed, make sure that whoever does the job knows how to introduce your guest Speakers correctly. Before that, he needs to begin the evening with some words of welcome. Something on these lines:

'Good evening, Ladies and Gentlemen, my name is Dougie Doings, and it's my pleasure to be your Compere this evening. As you are aware, the object of this event is to raise funds for DD Cricket Club, and there will be three fund-raisers during the course of the evening. We'd like you to contribute to the first two of them. Then at the end of the night there will be an auction when it's up to you if you participate or not.

'To start the ball rolling, our first fund-raiser is a lucky draw. In front of you you'll find a brown envelope and we'd like you to put a £5 note in the envelope, seal it and write your name on the front. Towards the end of the evening I will ask our special guest Dougie Doings to make the draw and the winner will receive a weekend for two in London with tickets to see 'Phantom of the Opera'. The value of the prize is £500, and we'd like to thank DD Travel for sponsoring the prize. Please have your £5 envelopes ready as four lovely girls are coming round to collect them very soon.

'During the sweet course, our four lovely girls will be back to encourage you to buy a few raffle tickets and there are 12 fabulous prizes, which I will announce later.

'Tonight we also have two of the finest sporting After Dinner Speakers in the country, and a fabulous Comedian who you probably saw on TV only last week.

'I know you're in for a fantastic night, and I am sure you will enjoy the meal.'

Let us analyse that introduction. Although there was an undercurrent of chatter in the room, every guest will have quickly done his calculations and assessed the night. He will have worked it out as follows:

'Three fund-raisers: a draw I can't get out of which will cost me £5, four girls who will encourage me to buy a few raffle tickets, maybe I can get away with a couple of quid. An auction – I'll miss that. A weekend for two in London – tickets for Phantom of the Opera – the wife will love that when I get home tonight. Finest After Dinner Speakers; Comedian off TV; fantastic night; enjoyable meal. At the worst, I'll get away with a tenner and have a chance of some great prizes.'

Your guest can now sit back and enjoy the night. He knows exactly what it will cost him, and just what he has got left to spend on a few drinks. Although only one prize has been announced, he has assessed that all the raffle prizes must be equally as good as the weekend in London ... and there is a good chance he will have something out of the 13 prizes to take home to his wife. Yes, the Compere is right, there is a great night in store.

Here is how not to do it:

'Tonight we're here to raise money. If we don't get over one thousand pounds out of you tonight, our Under-12s team with manager and coaches cannot go to America for 10 days this summer. So don't be tight, write your name on a £5 note ... and later on there's a raffle ... then a game of bingo ... then I want you all to put £5 into a glass ....'

The guests feel trapped, and worried that they are going to be ripped off. (For more details on the Draw, see Section 12.)

Introducing the Speaker

After the meal, the Compere needs to introduce your Speaker correctly. For a Speaker to perform to his or her full potential, the introduction is vitally important. A good Compere knows that the Speaker's introduction builds up to a crescendo, ending with the Speaker's name.

> 'I was once speaking at a dinner in Rochdale when the Master of Ceremonies – the brother of the event organiser – introduced an international footballer as follows (I have changed a few teams and towns to protect the innocent):
>
> "Now it's time to introduce one of our turns. Dougie Doings was once a top international footballer. He played for Bury, Blackpool [both teams wrong!] and finally Manchester United where he eventually got a free transfer. He's a local lad who couldn't manage to stay in football, so he now has a fish and chip shop in Accrington, and I'm sure if you are ever passing Dougie's shop he'll tell you he makes the best fish and chips in town.
>
> "So give 'im good order 'cos he's not used to this. Right, Dougie Doings, let's hear what you've got to say. [The Speaker then got to his feet.] Come on lads, lets hear you clap." '

As they say, there is nothing like a good build-down. Only a very experienced Speaker could handle an introduction like that.

Here is how a competent Compere would have introduced the same Speaker:

'It is now my pleasure to introduce to you our main celebrity guest. Following a spell at local clubs Blackburn Rovers and Manchester City, he joined Manchester United for a record fee in 1965. During his spell at the top club in British football at the time, he won 23 international caps under the great Alf Ramsey and was in the 1966 World Cup-winning squad. Following a fantastic career in football, he now is a successful businessman and has a restaurant not far from here in East Lancashire. Gentlemen, please welcome [pause] DOUGIE DOINGS.'

OK, maybe a few points have been exaggerated, but are the audience concerned? They have paid for a ticket to listen to some stories from an international footballer, not a chip shop owner!

IOT
When introducing your guest Speaker or Comedian,
never start off with the guest's name. These must be the
last words you use before your Speaker stands to speak:
'Ladies and Gentlemen, I am delighted to introduce ...
DOUGIE DOINGS!'

IOT
And never trust a special celebrity's name to memory.
Always, always write it down in large capital letters in
front of you if you are introducing them.

There are hundreds of examples of how not to introduce a celebrity Speaker.   Sometimes the stand-in amateur Compere, lubricated by too much drink to give himself false courage at the microphone, will try to get a cheap laugh on the back of his VIP special guest. Here are some examples:

'We're paying this lad a lot of money, so he'd better be good ... ha, ha, ha.'
'Let's see what Dougie Doings has written about himself ... ha, ha, ha.'
'It's now time to introduce Speaker ... [looks at the Speaker] what did you say your name was? Ha, ha, ha.'

It is only a very experienced Compere who can introduce a Speaker with insults. Sometimes a barrage of abuse can be an excellent introduction ... provided it comes from a professional Compere. Here is a sample introduction that Comedian Mike King often uses when he introduces me:

> 'Our Speaker started his career (for want of a better word) with Bolton
> Wanderers. In 1970 he joined Burnley for £166,000 and was one of the
> country's most expensive transfers. Burnley regretted every ******* penny!

After 10 years at Burnley, he was transferred to Blackpool for £60,000 when completely knackered. He then joined the infamous Colne Dynamos as Commercial Manager ... now they're completely knackered.

At present he is Chief Executive at the new Reebok Stadium, Bolton, following six years as Chief Executive of the Alfred McAlpine Stadium, Huddersfield. He's also a chartered accountant and tax advisor to Ken Dodd!

He also works weekends for Sky TV. No, not on the box .... He puts dishes on the sides of houses in Bolton!

Gentlemen, please welcome an ex-England international footballer who was a prolific goalscorer during the halcyon days of British football, now Chief Executive of the most expensive new Stadium ever built in the United Kingdom ... PAUL FLETCHER!'

The TIQS and T-CUT Method

To give an introduction a framework, the TIQS method is an excellent concept. It is used on Dale Carnegie 'Effective Human Relations' courses throughout the land. It stands for TOPIC, INTEREST (or importance), QUALIFY (or qualifications), SPEAKER. It works like this:

*   Begin the introduction by explaining the TOPIC the Speaker will be talking about.
*   Secondly, explain why this is of INTEREST or importance to the audience.
*   Thirdly, tell the audience why the Speaker is QUALIFIED to speak on the subject, and finally end with the SPEAKER'S name.

Here is how TIQS would work when introducing the superb football Speaker Tommy Docherty, one of the most experienced After Dinner Speakers in the country:

'Gentlemen, it gives me great pleasure to introduce to you our main Speaker this evening, who is from the World of Football (TOPIC). He has been involved in football for over 50 years as a Player, Coach, Manager and more recently as a TV and Radio Broadcaster (INTEREST). Starting his career with Preston North End in 1949, he went on to play for Arsenal and

Chelsea winning 25 Scotland caps along the way, and then went on to manage Chelsea, QPR (3 times), Aston Villa, Rotherham, Derby County, Hull, Manchester United, Preston, Wolves, Oporto and Sydney Olympic, and in 1974 took Scotland to the World Cup finals (QUALIFICATIONS). Gentlemen, please give a warm [name of local town] welcome to one of the biggest names in British Football ... TOMMY DOCHERTY (SPEAKER).'

Such is the power of this introduction and the depth of experience it contains, I have seen the audience give Tommy Docherty a standing ovation before he says a word. Respect indeed.

I have also heard the odd Compere end with the quip 'I only hold one thing against Tommy Docherty ... he didn't run off with my wife!' – which always gets a laugh.

After the Speech

A good Compere also understands the importance of thanking the Speaker at the end of his speech. It is far better to do this rather than simply letting the Speaker sit down, as many inexperienced Comperes do, which only leaves the audience wondering what is going to happen next.

Dale Carnegie uses the term T-CUT as a framework to say a thank-you to a Speaker as he sits down. It stands for THANK-YOU (from the Compere); CREDIT (the Speaker); U (what you the Compere liked); THANKS (from the audience).

Here is how the T-CUT would work at the Tommy Docherty dinner: 'Tommy, can I thank you for entertaining us with some wonderful stories this evening (THANK YOU from the Compere). You have had a magnificent career both as a footballer and football manager (CREDIT) and the story about your early days at Preston North End playing with Tom Finney stirred some wonderful memories not only for me but for many of us in the room this evening (U, one moment you the Compere liked about the speech). Gentlemen, please show your appreciation for our main Speaker this evening ... MR TOMMY DOCHERTY (THANKS from the audience).

Keeping the Speaker Informed

Most experienced Speakers ask the Compere how he will be introduced. Some even carry a photocopy of their own preferred form of introduction. If a Speaker or Comedian has been booked by an agent, the agent should be happy to send through a profile or career details of the Speaker/Comedian.

'In 1989 I was the main guest Speaker at a Sportsman's Dinner at the Piccadilly Hotel in Manchester. The function was a corporate dinner for the engineering industry and attended by around 250 guests from all over the country.

The organiser, a very abrupt officious individual in the Basil Fawlty mould, was treating me and the other Speaker (an international cricketer with over 50 Test caps) with an attitude verging on contempt. We were the "performing donkeys" who would jump to this master's command. But, as a couple of old pros, we got on with the evening and sat chatting to the other guests on the top table.

Halfway through dinner, I thought I would just check that "Basil" had an introduction for me. I thought I had better not risk "What did you say your name was?" from this clown, as it was now clear he was going to be the Compere and Master of Ceremonies – the self-styled centre of attraction for the night.

I quietly walked four places down the table and inquired about my introduction. He let me know in no uncertain terms that his brother, who was a football fan, had written down something about me that would suffice. Now would I "go and sit down". Tail between my legs, I returned to my seat. Then the warning bells started to ring, and I found I was not prepared to be embarrassed by this buffoon. So I wrote him a simple note and passed it down the top table.

"I'm sorry to be a pain, but I am not happy to speak this evening until I have seen how you intend to introduce me."

A few minutes later, a piece of A4 paper floated down on to my apple pie as Basil threw my introduction down the table while still talking to his chairman. As I read it, I felt cold with fear and warmed with delight, both at the same time. It read as follows:

"He used to play for Manchester City and started his career with his twin brother Ron at Luton. He played over...Paul Futcher."

A player from my era with a very similar surname. I waited until five minutes before I was due to speak, and sent him my second letter along the top table. It simply said: "I am not the person you are going to introduce! Good Luck."

Needless to say, I had a few derogatory things to say about Basil when I finally stood up (to a better introduction which I had written). He unwittingly even got a good laugh when he read out the teams I said I had played for: Bolton, Isle of Man St Joseph's, Burnley, Barcelona .... He even read out the line which said, "... he won four England caps in 1973 and also got a Dutch cap in Magaluf in 1982." '

Sometimes a Real Pro is Essential

Every so often, a dinner produces some acutely embarrassing moment which it needs something like genius to get round and defuse. This is a very special skill, and, if such a moment ever happened at your dinner, you would be extremely grateful if you had a quick-thinking, experienced Compere in charge of the microphone. It is one of those extra reasons to think seriously about booking a professional, rather than trying to skimp on costs by getting 'Old Dougie' to do it. Here is an example of the type of occasion I have in mind.

'I have only ever seen Compere Neil Midgley freeze on the microphone once! Neil is an ex-FIFA referee and one of the best Comperes in Britain. It was at Manchester United in the Banqueting Suite on a Saturday night in early 1990. The event was a mixed function for a local football team and the room was packed and the atmosphere superb. I had said my few words to a good response and Neil Midgley was up and down like the proverbial fiddler's elbow, entertaining, announcing, and taking the mickey out of the audience, many of whom he knew.

While he was on his feet, a young lad of about 23 in a wheelchair pushed himself past the top table and Neil had a word for him. "How are you, cocker? Nice to see our young friend here in the wheelchair. For those of you who don't know, Manchester United have excellent facilities for people with disabilities. Are you a United fan? [They had been beaten 2-1 at home that day] They could have done with you in the back four this afternoon, I'd back you over 10 yards with that Steve Bruce anyday."

It was just right. Not a bit offensive. And he treated the young man as people with disabilities should be treated, like everyone else. Everyone laughed at this witty, inoffensive joke, including the young man himself.

An hour later came the raffle. Neil asked me to give him a hand: "I'll shout the number, you tell me what they've won and pass it to me." The first few prizes went smoothly: "No 896, Blue ... Well done, sir, you've won a bottle of Scotch .... No 124, Buff, please come up and collect the next prize which is a ... Electric Teasmade ...' And so it went on. Midgley was in full flight, and the audience was bubbling.

There was one prize left: "No 238, Pink ... 238 Pink? Oh, it's my mate in the wheelchair. Get an early night tonight, you may get selected for United's first team next week – what's he won, Fletch?" It was the last prize, packed in a large heavy box. I started to read the label on the side. I went cold. It was a TROUSER PRESS!

As the young man made his way to the top table, Neil prompted me again, off microphone: "Come on, Fletch, stop messing about, what's he won?"

I didn't say a word, I just passed the large box to Neil. "Right, son. Congratulations. You've won a ... trouser press!"

For three seconds there was total silence. Then, God Bless him, the young man in the wheelchair started to laugh, and everyone else in the room laughed along with him. The night was saved. So was Neil. He was out of the mire and soon back in full flight.

"Can't life be a bastard? One minute you've nearly been selected for United's first team, next minute you've won yourself a ******* trouser press."

I don't know anyone who could have handled the situation so well.'

The Build-down

When creating a build-up for a Speaker, it is important not to make any negative announcements as part of the introduction. Any bad-luck story – about illness, death, theft, a fight, or something that sounds like a charity appeal – can instantly turn a build-up into its opposite, the proverbial 'build-down'. A good example of this comes from the heart of clubland in Sunderland. The venue and Speaker shall remain nameless.

> 'The Social Secretary, doubling up as a Master of Ceremonies for the night, introduced his guest Speaker as follows:
>
> "Before I introduce our Speaker this evening, I have an important announcement for all members. As you all know, the committee voted to award a cash sum of £200 to the family of any member who died during the year. So far this year we have paid out £1,200 and I have to announce that this money will stop at the end of March as the committee feel that some members are taking advantage.
>
> "That said, let me bring to the microphone tonight's guest Speaker ..." '

Mobile Phones

Mobile phones have become an essential nuisance. A train journey will never be the same for any of us as we sit amongst company executives or big-time charlies each of whom has programmed his own personal ringing tone. In fact you can nearly always assess the person by the way their mobile phone rings. The louder and longer the ring – the bigger the prat. That said, mobile phones are essential for many aspects of business and life in general. Especially when you are stuck on the M6 motorway in a line of traffic that is not moving.

At a Sportsman's Dinner, mobile phones are a particular headache, and nowadays a good Compere will always remind the audience about them. For example:

'Gentlemen, just in case you have forgotten to switch off your mobile phone, could you do it now out of courtesy to our Speakers and Comedian. Thank you.'

This not only reminds the guest who would have been extremely embarrassed if his phone had rung while the Speaker was on his feet, it also warns the idiot who has asked his wife to ring him at 10.15, just to show everyone in the room that he has got a new phone.

8
The Agent's Role

For many Sportsman's Dinners, the Compere, Comedian and Speaker (entertainer) are booked by an Agent on behalf of the organiser. Some Agents offer to do much more than this: they will help to organise the function, find sponsors, book caterers and so on. For his services, the Agent receives a fee, usually from the entertainer he books and which he collects directly from him after the event. An average fee is 10-20 per cent of what the entertainer is paid.

Advantages of Booking via an Agent

There are many advantages to booking your entertainer via an Agent. They are:

*   An Agent can give you a choice or list of entertainers to select from.

*   As it is the Agent who contacts the entertainer, this saves the organiser the trouble of locating, or finding out the telephone number of the entertainer.

*   An Agent will advise an organiser of the fee the entertainer charges. If this fee is too high, it is easy to say no to the Agent (it is more difficult to say no to a top celebrity Speaker once you have rung him at home). This obviously saves any haggling over fees.

*   It is the Agent's job to ensure that the entertainer attends the function. Usually he will provide him with the following information:

1 Date of event and time of arrival.

2 Type of function and type of organisation.

3 Gender of audience (male, mixed, etc).

4 How much the fee is, and how it will be paid, ie cash or cheque on the night or by invoice before or after the event.

5 Address of venue (often with directions).

6 Who the entertainer will be working with, ie which Speaker(s) or Comedian.

7 Contact name on arrival, with contact phone numbers should the entertainer wish to discuss the event with the organisers before he arrives.

8 Type of dress.

9 Special instructions.

A typical booking form looks something like the one shown opposite. To make things as clear as possible all round, it is useful if the Agent completes the form in triplicate and sends a copy to the entertainer and the organiser.

The Dinner Business
Dinner Business House
Cheadleswick
Cheshire

Telephone: 01661 888 8888
Fax: 01661 888 8889

CONFIRMATION OF BOOKING

Mr A D Speaker
Address and
postcode

Date

DATE OF FUNCTION	15 September 1999
TYPE	Rugby Club Annual Dinner
TIME	7.30pm for 8.00pm
DRESS	Lounge suit
GUESTS/GENDER	250/male
CONTACT	Dougie Doings 01254 849876 (H)
COMPERE	Dougie Doings
COMEDIAN	Dougie Doings
ACCOMMODATION	n/a
MAP	Enclosed
FEE AGREED	£750.00 cash/cheque less 15% – paid on night
EXTRA INFORMATION	Team has won Championship. Captain has scored 25 tries.

Many thanks.

Dougie Doings
The Dinner Business

Please retain one copy and sign and return one copy to The Dinner Business at the above address.
I accept the engagement as detailed above and agree to pay The Dinner Business a commission of 15% of the fee quoted.

SIGNED...**DATE**....................

Notes

*   Sometimes an Agent will book an entertainer via a formal contract, and send a copy to the event organisers. This may be a standard VAEC (Variety and Allied Entertainment's Council) Contract.

*   If a celebrity entertainer is booked via an Agent, this is usually a guarantee that he will attend the function. On very rare occasions, there are genuine reasons which prevent the entertainer from attending, eg illness, misunderstanding of dates, delays due to transport (car, plane or rail) or accident. In these circumstances an Agent can usually be contacted until late in the evening and can be expected to find a replacement within the hour.

*   Agents can also find replacements should an entertainer cancel the engagement in advance of the event for whatever reason.

*   Comedians sometimes attend a function after the meal. Either they, or their Agent, should inform the organiser of this.

*   The Terms and Conditions when booking via an Agent may include the clause 'Professional Engagements Permitting'. This covers many celebrity and personality Speakers who are under permanent management contracts with companies such as the BBC, SKY, ITV, Sporting Clubs, Theatres, etc. On very rare occasions this clause may have to be invoked because your star celebrity Speaker has been called away before the event. Most Agents undertake to provide a first-class replacement.

Disadvantages of Booking via an Agent

*   The organiser may feel he could pay the entertainer a smaller fee by booking him direct. This saves the Speaker the Agent's fee.

*   Some unscrupulous Agents have been known to inflate a Speaker's fee grossly and invoice the organiser direct. For example, if the

Speaker usually charges £500, the Agent asks for £1,000, makes £500 for himself and still receives 15% commission from the Speaker. Unless the Speaker asks the organiser what fee was requested by his Agent, he will not realise he has been hired at an inflated fee.

* Some organisers enjoy the personal satisfaction of ringing a top celebrity direct to make all the arrangements, rather than meet him 'cold' for the first time on the night.

* The Agent's contract may stipulate compensation should the organiser cancel the event. For example, if the organiser cancels 4 weeks prior to the event, 50% of the fee is payable; 3 weeks, 60%; 2 weeks, 75%, and 1 week or less, 100%.

Although these terms and conditions are covered in writing on an Agent's contract or booking sheet, sometimes Speakers are able to hold organisers to a verbal contract should an event be cancelled, irrespective of whether the Speaker was booked via an Agent or direct. Many Speakers are members of Equity, and the union's solicitors are often successful at winning compensation.

The Entertainer-Agent Relationship

Even if an entertainer has been booked via an Agent, most entertainers like to be paid directly by the organiser on the night. It has been known for some organisers to pay the Agent and the Agent not to pass on the money to the entertainer.

Some entertainers will work solely for one agent. Even if an organisation books them direct via their home telephone, the entertainer will still pass on to an agent a percentage of their fee.

Agents will, on occasions, book an entertainer via another agent. They will either agree to split the fee, or each will charge their normal fee, thereby inflating the price of the entertainer.

As mentioned, some entertainers are members of Equity and their Agents may use the Equity booking form (or VAEC Contract) which has many detailed contractual obligations for both parties. It is as well to read the details carefully prior to signing this contract, so that you are aware of your obligations should either party default.

IOT
**Understand the implications of a legal contract before
you sign it.**

To sum up, the role of the Agent works very well. Agents play an important part in event organisation and provide a valuable service.

9
The Ticket

The ticket may not seem important, but it is. Apart from giving precise information to your guests, it can set the scene for the event itself. Each ticket bears the unwritten signature of the organiser. A cheap, badly printed, uninformative ticket suggests a cheap, badly organised event. Do not scrimp on the ticket, printed menu or any of your stationery. And remember, with the ticket you only have one chance to make a good first impression. That said, here is the rest of the information it is important to include.

Checklist

1 Title of event
2 Venue: name, address and telephone number
3 Reason/beneficiary
4 Date
5 Start/finish times
6 Dress
7 Ticket price

Optional

8 Speaker/Comedian/Compere
9 Guest of Honour
10 Sponsorship information
11 Numbering
12 Printing options on reverse
13 Photographs
14 Colour
15 Logos.

£MT
Do not forget Palermo's Law: 'Check twice, print once'.
In other words, a simple mistake on your ticket or the
omission of vital information (eg date of function) could
result in either a costly reprint or numerous phonecalls.

The Checklist in Detail

1 Title of Event

It is essential to state clearly whether the function is an all-male event or a mixed function. Should the event be all-male, it is important to state 'Sportsman's Dinner'. A verbal explanation must also be given when tickets are being sold, especially to sponsors who would be embarrassed if they arrived at the function (with their wife) thinking it is a mixed event.

2 Venue

When stating the name and address of the venue it is an excellent idea to include the telephone number plus area code. This is to help the guests or entertainers who may wish to ring the venue, either in advance or on the night, to speak to the organiser, check directions, send messages about late arrivals, check accommodation possibilities (hotels only), ask about vegetarian meals, etc. Many people now carry mobile phones or have car phones. If a guest has a problem on his way to the function, and needs to contact the organiser or venue, this information will be invaluable to him.

3 Reason/Beneficiary

It is easy to forget to include the reason for the function on the ticket. State this clearly, whether it is on behalf of the Dougie Doings Testimonial, a School PTA, Dougie Doings Football Club, DD Charity raising funds for Dougie Doings, and so on.

4 Date

Write it in full in this order, without abbreviations, eg Tuesday 2 November 1999.

5 Start/Finish Times

Traditionally, guests are asked to arrive during a period of 30 minutes before the official start time, eg 'Reception 7.30 for 8.00'. Although the majority of guests will arrive during this period, about 10 per cent will arrive between 7.55 and 8.15.

On arrival, most guests walk directly to the bar, where they expect to find their party or friends, to order a drink. As the bar will be at its most congested between 7.45 and 8.00, late guests delay matters even further as they tag on the end of the queue for drinks.

Some tips to improve punctuality:

a) State the start time on the ticket, eg '7.30 Reception for 8.00 prompt start'.

b) Tell the kitchen that they must be ready to start serving sometime between 8.00 and 8.15.

c) Make an announcement at 7.50 asking guests to take their seats for dinner. This encourages guests standing around the bar to move into the function room and free the bar area for the late arrivals. By starting at 8.15, all late-comers will have been given 15 minutes' grace, but they will not have delayed the smooth running of the evening which, if at all possible, should finish on time, or, at the very worst, within 30 minutes of the time stated on the ticket. If your guests have arranged to be picked up at the finish time stated on the ticket, they will be annoyed if the function finishes late.

6 Dress

There are various options:

a) Smart Casual = A collar and tie is not necessary but no jeans or trainers.

b) Lounge Suit = A collar, tie and jacket.

c)   Formal/Evening Suit/Dinner Jacket/Black Tie = Evening suit and bow tie.

d)   Optional = Either lounge suit or evening suit.

e)   Evening Suit or Dark Suit with Bow Tie = Anyone who does not have an evening suit just needs to wear a bow tie with a dark suit.

f)   Old School Tie, Fancy Bow Tie, etc. = exactly what it says, plus a suit.

State one of these options clearly on the ticket.

7 Ticket Price
Always state the individual ticket price on the ticket. (See Section 2 'The Budget' for VAT implications.)

8 Speaker/Comedian/Compere
Celebrity entertainers help to sell tickets, so make sure you mention them on the ticket.

9 Guest of Honour
As above. If your guest of honour will help to sell tickets, mention him on the ticket.

10 Sponsorship Information
If a Sponsor has been found at an early stage before tickets are printed, it is a good opportunity to advertise this on the front of the ticket. You may also wish to offer the Sponsor the back of the ticket as part of the package.

11 Numbering
Some organisations have each ticket numbered to hold a free 'ticket draw' on the night. As, usually, only 50 per cent of attendees bring their ticket along this can be risky.

12 Printing Options on Reverse
The back of the ticket can be used in various ways, for example to:

a) Advertise for the sponsor

b) Sell to an alternative advertiser

c) Give details of how to get to the venue, including map

d) Explain the event or beneficiary in more detail

e) Carry a photograph of the Star Celebrity Speaker which he can autograph. (He'll love you for this if you sell 500 tickets!)

13 Photographs
Black-and-white or colour photographs will always enhance your ticket. Alternatively, a photograph can be printed on, or form part of, a tinted background.

14 Colour
Each additional colour increases cost, but adds to quality.

15 Logos
Sponsors' logos, club crests, badges and mottoes can all add to the appearance of a ticket.

Proof Reading is Essential
Proof reed carfully for spellling mistackes. Also ask a coleague to prof read also. A mistak on the ticket will either be embarasing or kostly.

Summary
The ticket should reflect the event. Quality stock, quality information, quality printing ... equals a Quality function.

10
The Menu

The Menu (or event brochure) is another opportunity to indicate to your guests the standard of evening you are trying to achieve. A white photocopied menu card, folded badly, lets your guests know that you are running the event 'on the cheap'. However, a quality menu on good printing stock, with a ribbon which matches either the club colours or the room décor, sets the scene for a quality evening.

The financial difference between the above two menus amounts to a few pounds. Looked at another way, do not think you can make a saving by setting out a cheap and nasty menu – it is a false economy.

For an indication of how good your menu is, take a look around the room once your event is over. The amount of menus taken by your guests will indicate how many felt it was worth retaining as a memento of the night.

Menus can range from the sublime to the ridiculous, from novelty ones the size of a business card at a referees' dinner (who says they need glasses?) right up to a full-colour 72-page brochure costing many thousands of pounds to produce.

More common is the A4 Astralux card, which has a high-gloss coloured exterior and plain white interior, folded in half to give an A5 menu with four printed pages. These are usually laid out as follows:

Page One	Front cover, with information about the event
Page Two	Menu
Page Three	Running order, information about Speakers, etc
Page Four	Back cover, a utility page containing, for example:

    a)   List of sponsors
    b)   Autographs
    c)   Details of the beneficiary (charity organisation or testimonial)
    d)   Advertising.

Let us look at these in more detail:

Page One – Checklist for Front Cover

1 Insert the full date, as on the ticket
2 Title of the event
3 Venue (name only)
4 Sponsors' information if applicable.

There are some examples of all four menu pages at the end of this chapter. The Blackburn Lions' Sportsman's Evening menu is, by the way, the only one I have come across with a space on the front for the guest's name. If such menus are placed beside each table setting before the meal, as is the usual practice, this does without the need for separately printed place cards.

Page Two – The Menu in Detail

Here it is best to go for simplicity. Keep this page clear of all other material and print your menu, course by course, with plenty of white space around it and perhaps a piece of decorative type to separate one course from another.

Most dinner menus adopt the style of a straightforward restaurant menu – but there is nothing to stop you writing your own for a bit of fun:

MENU

The Chairman's
Spring Vegetable Soup
(colourful but thick)

*****

The Mad Cow Special
Roast Beef and Yorkshire Pudding
(sponsored by the team captain, the mad
cow himself, Dougie Doings)
with Roast and Boiled Potatoes,
Carrots and Peas

*****

The Club Secretary's Pudding
(no it's not his girlfriend!)
Apple Pie and Cream

*****

The Treasurer's Delight
Coffee and Mints
(sounds expensive – costs little)

Page Three – The Running Order in Detail

This is the place to credit those who will take an active part in your dinner: by saying Grace, proposing the Loyal Toast, making the announcements and ensuring the evening runs smoothly (the Compere), and, of course, the Speaker(s) and Comedian who have come to entertain your guests.

When listing your Speakers, it is important not to list them as 'First' or 'Second' Speaker.

Many Speakers prefer to decide for themselves on the night who should go first. Usually the stronger Speaker goes second, irrespective of whether or not he is the big name. Many Top Celebrities are not particularly good Speakers and their job is made twice as hard (and can be twice as embarrassing) if they have to follow a first Speaker who has had the audience falling off their chairs with laughter.

Also, do not put timings on your menu. If things start running behind time, it is not a good idea to let everyone know how disorganised you are.

Page Four – Back Cover Contents in Detail

a) List of Sponsors
Should your table Sponsors be using the night for corporate entertaining, and putting the costs through their company books as sponsorship, advertising or hospitality, they may need evidence that these elements were included. By listing the Sponsors' names on the menu, and making sure that they are mentioned and thanked by the Compere, you will ensure that the event is classed as legitimate company expenditure.

I always think it is a nice touch when a Compere suggests to the audience: 'If ever the opportunity arises to pass on some business to any of tonight's Sponsors, then their investment this evening will have been worthwhile.'

b) Autographs
The more famous the Celebrity Speaker or Guest of Honour, the more people will want his autograph. At the end of the night, the tipsy guest will not only want to take home the celebrity's signature, but also to remind him of that match in 1954 when 'England needed 62 from the last four overs ... and I took my son who now lives in Chester with two children, Bill and Beryl ... Bill's going to play cricket just like you ... and Beryl has just started school ... do you remember that match?' Yes, you would be amazed at some of the questions the famous are asked ... and meanwhile the queue gets longer and longer ... 'and then you come in to bat. I said to young Bill we only need 23 runs to win and there is no better player in the country to do it' ... and the queue gets longer ... 'and the bowler ran up ...'

Autographs and a brief chat with the famous are certainly all part of the night. But it is a good idea to top and tail the evening by having the Compere announce that 'Your special guest would be delighted to sign autographs for a short period at the end of the meal.' Rest assured, there will still be a steady flow of autograph-hunters throughout the night, irrespective of this announcement. But at least the queue will not be as long.

So, if you think the demand will be there, leave a special panel for 'Autographs' on Page Four of your menu.

IOT

Do not let your VIP guest be overwhelmed by autograph hunters.

c) The Beneficiary

It is sometimes a good idea to let all the guests know exactly where the profits from the night are going. I have been to dinners at professional football clubs where the concept of the evening is to raise funds for the 'Youth Development Scheme'. Yet I am sure all proceeds were going directly into the club's coffers, from where, maybe, some of it eventually filtered down towards the Youth Policy.

Certainly, to announce a 'favoured beneficiary' is far better than letting the audience assume that all proceeds will go towards helping to pay players' wages. You can do this with a simple notice in your menu-programme.

d) Advertising

Page Four is probably the best space to concentrate your advertising. Remember, too, that it is often possible to have the menus paid for by an advertiser, or a number of advertisers. If your menu is a quality production and will possibly be autographed by an international celebrity, it will make a great souvenir. It will also be seen by far more people than the number of guests who attend the function.

You can easily make the list of the advertisers who would be keen for exposure to your audience. Here are some suggestions:

*   Local taxi company – some of your guests may use the telephone number later that evening.
*   Printer – the menu is an example of his work.
*   Sports Shop that supplies the team – advertising helps them to retain the alliance.
*   Banks, Building Societies, Estate Agents – great exposure for them, especially if the manager is in the audience and gets a personal mention on the night.
*   A new business, say a restaurant owner or publican who needs to get accepted locally.
*   A Player, Club Director or Committee Member who has a business in the area.

The simple formula is:

1   Make up a dummy menu.
2   Get a quote for the cost of printing.
3   Work out how much space you have got for advertising, eg one and a half or two pages, and how you can divide this up into full, half and quarter pages.
4   Sell this advertising for the same amount as the menu will cost to print.

£MT
Get your menu sponsored.

Obviously, it is not possible to sell this space if you have offered it to your main sponsor as part of his package. But this does not stop you adding pages to your menu.

Looking for a Sponsor?

If your organisation is looking for a Sponsor or sponsorship, the menu could be an ideal opportunity to list the benefits of your sponsorship package. On quite a few occasions I have been to dinners where the organisers have announced that they are looking for a main sponsor. It is always a nice surprise when it is announced later in the evening that DD Computer Company has agreed to sponsor the team for the next year.

£MT
If you are looking for a sponsor, advertise your package
on your menu.

Below is a sample notice listing the deals of a sponsorship package:

'If your company is looking for brand-name exposure all around this area, next season our main sponsorship is available. Your company's name would be featured on:

* **All team shirts (4 teams) and tracksuits**
* **Team coach**
* **All match programmes and event tickets**

We also offer:

* **6 tickets to the Chairman's Annual Dinner**
* **5000 free tickets to every match**
* **4 perimeter boards around the pitch.**

Over 20,000 opposing players and spectators will see the team play in the DD League, which features 15 teams in each League, and during the course of a season your company's name will get massive exposure. This season the team's photograph with sponsored shirts has been pictured in the (name of newspaper) on 12 occasions.

For more details, please ring our Commercial Manager Dougie Doings on ... [phone number].'

On a cold Monday morning this package could be difficult to sell to a potential Sponsor. His telephone is ringing, his secretary is sick, the letters are piling up high and budgets are tight. But, as a guest at a Sportsman's Dinner, without these pressures, warmed by a few glasses of good red wine, the local businessman often cannot resist when his host shouts across the table: 'Dougie, this sponsorship package could just be right for you. Your company is getting bigger and bigger and you need to start spreading your name around the community ... where's that Commercial Manager?'

£MT
Sign up the deal on the night.

Announce the sponsorship on the night and take a photograph of a signing ceremony on the top table (your Celebrity Guest will be pleased to shake your new Sponsor's hand). It is important to do this because on Monday morning the concept might not seem such a good idea, as the telephone is ringing, the secretary is sick, and so on.

The Testimonial Dinner is covered in a separate section, but when you are considering the menu, if the function is being run by a testimonial committee on behalf of a sportsperson, it is a good idea to carry a photograph of the recipient with some career details. And, of course, leave some space for an autograph.

AFAR – the Referral Slip

One thing I have not seen in a menu or evening programme is a referral slip. Many companies nowadays use referrals as a marketing tool; it is a concept that works much better than cold calling or other forms of scattergun advertising.

As they say, 'If you want to go AFAR, Ask For A Referral'. There is a story about a salesman who had the four letters 'AFAR' printed in raised metallic letters, which he then stuck on the handle of his briefcase. From then on, he could always feel the letters as he picked up his briefcase to leave a sales presentation, and they always reminded him to Ask for a Referral, irrespective of whether he had completed a sale.

The referral concept can work well on a menu if it includes an incentive. For example:

'If you have enjoyed tonight's function and can recommend any colleagues who you feel would benefit from attending, sponsoring, or taking a corporate table at our next function, please complete the form below. Just to say thanks, we will be pleased to send you two tickets to our next home match (or a bottle of wine, a signed football or cricket bat, etc).'

Sample Referral Slip

Your Name: . . . . .Company: . . . .
Colleague's Name: . . . . .Company: . . . .
Title: . . . .
Address: . . . .
. . . .
. . . .
Tel . . . .

If it really has been a great evening, make sure that your Compere mentions your referral slip at the end of the function.

Remember to deliver by hand the match tickets or bottle of wine, etc, for each referral slip that is returned. This will give you the opportunity not only to pencil in the referrer for the next dinner, but he may also give you a few other names if you ask him nicely.

Summary of Dos and Don'ts

Here is a summary of things that will make your menu stand out from the crowd:

1   Full colour
2   Unusual shape (football, rugby ball, etc)
3   Ribbons
4   Gold foil printing
5   Dye-stamping
6   Good graphic design
7   Quality printing stock

Here are some things that will have the same effect but for all the wrong reasons:

1   Photocopying rather than printing
2   Spellling mistaks
3   Gold edge (commonly used for wedding stationery)
4   Too big (does not fit in a pocket or has to be folded)
5   Poor-quality printing stock
7   Hand-written or typewriter-written.

More Menu Ideas

There is of course a multitude of information you could include in your menu-programme. Here is a list of ideas from more than 2000 menus collected over the past 10 years:

1   Chairman's or Captain's Welcome or President's Address
2   Wine list prices (if paying corkage)
3   Club history
4   Ex-players (who began at the club) – 'Where are they now?'
5   Club crest
6   Club honours list
7   Photographs: team, manager, star players, speakers, etc
8   A sporting poem

9   Club song
10 Forthcoming events
11 Information about the next dinner
12 List of past managers, chairmen, presidents
13 List of raffle prizes or auction Items
14 Write-up on your Speakers, Comedian, Compere
15 Seating plan by name (Who's Who)
16 Club address, telephone number, web site
17 League tables, current or past
18 Colemanballs
19 Club statistics: appearances, goalscorers, etc
20 A thank-you
21 Cartoon
22 Old programme cover (or extract from old programme)
23 Match report (newspaper cutting)
24 Guess the length of the speech.

Colemanballs

To add a bit of spice to your menu, why not include a few 'Colemanballs'. These are a few I have collected over the years:

- 'For those watching in black and white, City are wearing the light-blue shirts.'
- 'And with the last kick of the game, McDonald scored with a header.'
- 'Richie has now scored 11 goals, doubling his tally of last season.'
- 'And now a familiar sight, Liverpool raising the League Cup for the very first time.'
- '... the Arsenal defender is skating close to the wind.'
- 'Platini was given a great reception when he went off.'
- 'I don't think cricket should be used as a political football.'
- 'Newcastle, of course, are unbeaten in their last five wins.'
- 'Beckenbauer really has gambled all his eggs this time.'
- 'Celtic Manager David Hay still has a fresh pair of legs up his sleeve.'
- 'He's watching us from his hospital bed with his injured right knee.'
- 'If Derby score before half-time, the glove will be on the other foot.'

- 'Even though Everton have a man sent off, Chelsea have had an extra man for all the game.'
- 'There's only one thing that can now end this game .... the final whistle.'
- 'Although we're only 10 minutes into the match, I can tell you this game's a long way from being over.'
- 'There are three things that matter in this game. Scoring and keeping the score.'

Poems and Inspirational Quotations

These can also work well, placed somewhere appropriate in your menu.

For example:

A Woman's Lament
He's football crazy,
He's football mad,
The football game has taken away
The wee bit of sense he had.
It would take a dozen skivvies
His clothes to wash and scrub,
Since father became a member
Of the Terrible Football Club.

If You Think
If you think you are beaten, you are.
If you think you dare not, you don't.
If you like to win but think you can't,
It's almost certain that you won't.
Life's battles don't always go
To the stronger woman or man,
But sooner or later, those who win
Are those who think they can.

Life's a Game
So you've played the game and lost, my lad,
And you're battered and bleeding too,
And your hopes are dead and your heart is lead,
And your whole world is sad and blue,
And you sob and cry, in grief and pain,
For the hopes that had to die,
But the game is through and it's up to you,
To laugh though you want to cry.

For someone has to lose, my lad
It's sad, but it's always true,
And day by day in the games you play,
It's sometimes sure to be you,
So grit your teeth to the pain, my lad,
For you battled the best you could,
And there's never shame in losing the game,
When you lose like a real man should.

For after all life's a game, my lad,
And we play, as best we may,
We win or lose, as the gods may choose,
Who govern the games we play,
But whether we win or lose, my lad,
At the end, when the battle's through,
We must wait with a smile for after a while,
The chances will come anew.

School Songs
I am thinking in particular of Schools Dinners, but any song that is closely associated with the hosts for the evening can be worth its place in the menu.

Here are two rousing examples:

School Song 'Rio'
I've never sailed the Amazon
I've never reached Brazil
But the Don and the Magdalena
They go there when they will
Ah – ah, ah-ah, ah!
Yes, weekly from Southampton
Great steamers, white and gold
Go rolling down to Rio
Roll down, roll down to Rio
And I'd like to roll to Rio
Some day before I'm old
To roll
I'd like to roll to Rio
Some day before I'm old.

I've never seen a jaguar
Nor yet an armadillo
Dillowing in his amour
I s'pose I never will
Ah – ah, ah-ah, ah!
Unless I go to Rio
These wonders to behold
Go rolling down to Rio
Roll down, roll down to Rio
I'd like to roll to Rio
Some day before I'm old
To roll
I'd like to roll to Rio
Some day before I'm old.

The School Song

Beloved School, to thee we raise
With joyful hearts our song of praise
Whene'er our thoughts to thee are turned
We'll offer thanks for all we've learned.

Floreat Schola, Floreat Schola,
Floreat Schola, Almondburiensis

Here stood, as ancient records state
A Chantry School at Saint Helen's Gate
For this our song of thanks we'll sing:
In praises loud our voices ring:

Floreat Schola, Floreat Schola,
Floreat Schola, Almondburiensis

A charter granted by King James
Restored the school with loftier aims
To him our gratitude is due
For him our praises we'll renew.

Floreat Schola, Floreat Schola,
Floreat Schola, Almondburiensis

O dearest School, beneath whose shade
Our childhood games we oft have played
Though from your care we must depart
We yet will sing with joyful heart.

Floreat Schola, Floreat Schola,
Floreat Schola, Almondburiensis.

THE TIGER REVIEW

TURTON
FOOTBALL CLUB
Season 1993/94

Members of the John Smith's West Lancashire Football League

**CLUB
SPONSORS**

R SE
COUNTY
W I N D O W S
L I M I T E D

HENRY KNOTT
ASSOCIATES
LIMITED

SPORTSMAN'S DINNER
Wednesday November 10th 1993
At Bolton Town Hall

178

Sponsored by
PETER JAMES PACKAGING

OFFICIAL MATCHDAY PROGRAMME

50p

SALE MOOR CRICKET CLUB

Sportsmans Dinner

21st March 1996

Lancashire County Cricket Club

Trafford Suite, Old Trafford M16 0PX

GUEST SPEAKERS

Paul Fletcher – FORMER BURNLEY F.C.

Mike Lancaster – COMEDIAN

Norman Vernon – COMPERE

F.T.F.C.

Felixstowe Town Football Club

Dellwood Avenue, Felixstowe, Suffolk

(Founded 1890)

ARE PROUD TO
PRESENT

The Sixth Suffolk Sportsman's Dinner

THURSDAY 31st MARCH 1994

IPSWICH MOAT HOUSE
COPDOCK

Felixstowe Town F.C. would like to acknowledge the following for their continued support and sponsorship

FRED OLSEN AGENCIES LTD.

SPECIALISED FIXINGS (EAST ANGLIA) LTD.

P&O EUROPEAN FERRIES (FELIXSTOWE LTD)

MARITIME CARGO PROCESSING P.L.C.

Blackburn
Lions

Sportsman's Evening

to be held on

FRIDAY 24th APRIL, 1998

at

BLACKBURN COUNTY HOTEL

7.00 p.m. for 7.30 p.m.

Speaker
Paul Fletcher

Comedian
Tom Pepper

Paul Fletcher

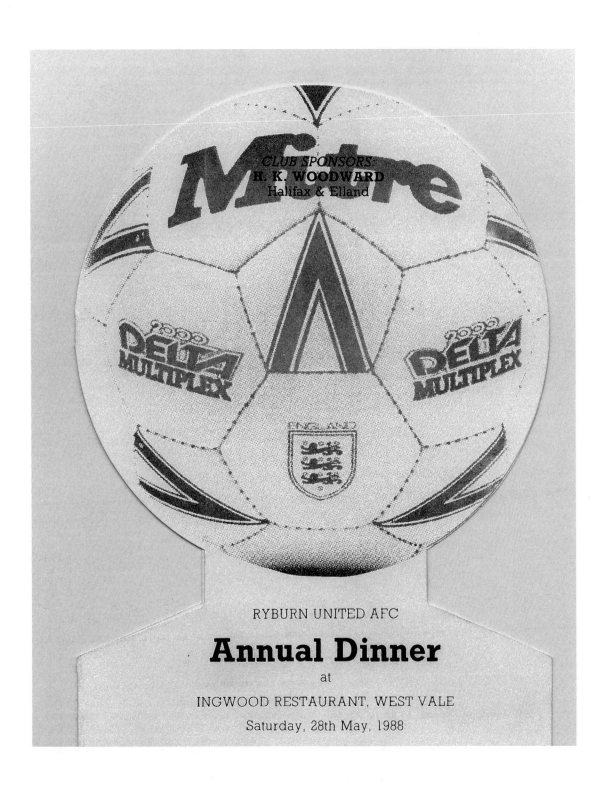

CLUB SPONSORS:
H. K. WOODWARD
Halifax & Elland

RYBURN UNITED AFC

Annual Dinner

at

INGWOOD RESTAURANT, WEST VALE

Saturday, 28th May, 1988

F.T.F.C.

GRACE
MR. PAUL BRIGGINSHAW
Managing Director, Fred Olsen Agencies Ltd.

MENU

Hearty Ham and Lentil Soup
Served with Crunchy Cheese Croutons

* * *

Roast Norfolk Turkey with Sage and Sausage Forcemeat
Bacon Rolls and Cranberries

* * *

Chefs Selection of Vegetables

* * *

Belgian Apple and Sultana Lattice Flan
or
Cheese, Biscuits and Celery

* * *

Coffee and Mints

THE LOYAL TOAST
MR. CHARLES WILKINSON
Chief Executive, Maritime Cargo Processing P.L.C.

Gentlemen, please refrain from smoking until after the Loyal Toast

The Banquet

Minestrone Soup

✤✤✤

Fish Mornay

✤✤✤

Roast Beef Chasseur
served with
Roast Potatoes and Seasonal Vegetables

✤✤✤

Fresh Fruit Salad
or
Gateau

✤✤✤

Cheese and Biscuits

✤✤✤

Coffee and Mints

TURTON F.C.   **SEASON 1993 ~ '94**

TO ~NIGHT'S MENU·

Tasty Scotch Broth
with soft roll and butter

o0o

Oven Roasted Breast of Chicken
sprinkled with Italian Herbs
and served with Sage and Onion Seasoning

Accompanied by a Selection of Market Fresh Vegetables and Potatoes

o0o

Tradition Homemade Apple Pie with Fresh Cream

o0o

Freshly Brewed Coffee or Tea with Mint Wafers

JUNIOR SPONSORS

DARWEN INDUSTRIAL SERVICES
Sunnybank Works ~ Hannah Street ~ Darwen ~ Lancs BB3 3HL
Tel: (0254) ~ 774119 Fax: (0204) ~ 771211

P.S.E.C.
Public Sector Management Consultants
021~585~5701

BEAUMONT HOSPITAL

MENU

Minestrone Soup

Fresh Vegetables, Tomato, Pasta and Garlic

* * *

Roast Beef and Yorkshire Pudding

*Thick Sliced Roast Beef with
Freshly Made Yorkshire Pudding
and Horseradish Sauce*

* * *

Cheese and Biscuits

*Fresh White Cheddar and Stilton Cheese
with a Selection of Biscuits*

* * *

Coffee and Mints

* * *

What's to Eat

Melon Boat from t'sea
❧
Redwell Beefy Bits with a sort of
sauce on them.
Other Non-Beefy Bits come
in a seperete dish.
❧
Black Forest Gatto
with cream if you want some
❧
Chees & Biscuits together
❧
Coffee & Toffee

Clean plates get a lolly
❧
After this dinner the staff all go to
the home for the bewildered -
Grange-o-Sands

Third time very lucky for our
Thursday Club Members. Tonight,
a wealth of oratorial talent is
present. Sadly, they are members of
the audience.

Our top table tonight along with
our sponsors comprise two lesser
mortals. They will however not be
on their feet long enough to spoil
the evening

They are:-
Paul Fletcher:
Short talk
&
Mike King:
Short talk but will seem longer.

Both Burnley lads but at least
they've got their health!

PROGRAMME

Compere,
Neil Midgley

Grace,

The Loyal Toast

Guest Speaker,
Paul Fletcher

Comedian,
Trevor "Sid the Parrot" James

Comedian
Max Pressure

ORDER OF EVENTS

Grace
Given by H. F. Bullough
President of Wigan Cricket Club

The Loyal Toast
Proposed by H. F. Bullough
President of Wigan Cricket Club

GUEST SPEAKER:
Paul Fletcher
(ex Burnley F.C.)

COMEDIAN:
Johnny Casson

M.C.
Johnny Casson

Guest Speakers
and Master of Ceremonies

Master of Ceremonies:
Mr. MURRAY BIRNIE

Guest Speaker:
MR. PAUL FLETCHER
*When Paul Fletcher joined 1st Division Burnley in 1969
for £166,000, he became one of the 1st Division's most expensive players.
During the next ten years he made over 400 appearances, mostly in the 1st Division.
He gained 4 U23 International caps but was prevented from joining
Don Revie's full England squad, by a serious knee injury.
He became Chief Executive of Huddersfield Town F.C in 1991 and is
also a Consultant to the P.F.A..*

Guest Speaker
Mr. VINCE EARL
Comedian & T.V.'s Ron Dixon from Brookside.

All the Directors & Staff of
REDROW HOMES Northern Limited
*wish everyone a very pleasant evening and
would like to thank them for their support & donations.*

LOYAL TOAST
Proposed by the President, Mike Whelan Esq.

TOAST
Burtonwood Brewery Manchester and District Cricket Association
Proposed by
Bob Taylor Esq. MBE. (Derbyshire and England)

RESPONSE
The President, Mike Whelan Esq.

PRESENTATION OF TROPHIES

TOAST TO THE GUESTS
Proposed by the President, Mike Whelan Esq.

RESPONSE ON BEHALF OF THE GUESTS
Paul Fletcher Esq. (Bolton Wanderers and Burnley)

MASTER OF CEREMONIES
Frank Bailey Esq.

Chairmans Message

On behalf of the Branch Committee, I would like to thank you for your support at this our Annual Dinner of the East Midlands Branch of the Coal Trade Benevolent Association.

There are some who believe C.T.B.A. is only about money, but this is only half the story. It is about people and people caring about people in this materialistic world we live in. Can you put a price on a smile, or words of comfort, when helping to ease the problems of those less fortunate than ourselves.

Your generosity here tonight will enable us to continue the help we give our beneficiaries throughout the year ahead.

Thank you for coming tonight. I wish you a most enjoyable evening.

MICHAEL TAYLOUR
(East Midlands Branch Chairman)

CAPTAIN'S MESSAGE

Welcome to the Thirteenth Sportsman's Dinner.
As always I am sure you will have an enjoyable evening.
Official duties prevent me from being here in person, but my
grateful thanks go to you all for your support in this fund
raising evening. Particular thanks to those of you who have
supported us in past years and continue to do so.
Finally, my grateful thanks to John Ankers and his team for
their time and effort in putting the night together.

Gentlemen enjoy your evening.

Oscar Goldstein
Captain

TONIGHTS SPECIAL RAFFLE

TICKETS £5 EACH

We pride ourselves in giving value for money in appreciation of your attendance at tonight's function. The numerous prizes are varied and very acceptable. We hope you win one of the following:-

1st Prize 14" Colour T.V., kindly donated by Les Miller

2nd Prize 5 Day Mini Cruise to Belgium for 2 people and car, including 1 nights accommodation for 2 in Brugges at 3 star hotel, P&O European Ferries (Felixstowe) Ltd

3rd Prize Moulinex Microwave, kindly donated by Les Miller

4th Prize £100 Marks & Spencer vouchers, kindly donated by Fred Olsen Agencies Ltd

5th Prize Weekend for two at the Bournemouth Moat House, donated by Ipswich Moat House

6th Prize CD Walkman, kindly donated by Maritime Cargo Processing P.L.C.

7th Prize Dartington Crystal decanter and glasses, and a bottle of malt whisky, donated by Mr D. Haddow

8th Prize Three cases of claret (18 bottles), kindly donated by Mr B. Gould

9th Prize A selection of malt whisky's, courtesy of F.T.F.C.

10th Prize A collection of 10 CD's, kindly donated by Chilvers Automatics Ltd

11th Prize A bottle of malt whisky, kindly donated by Mr P. Catchpole

12th Prize Bouquet of flowers, kindly donated by Fruit & Veg (East Anglia) Ltd

Plus various mystery prizes

TONIGHTS AUCTION

1. AUTOGRAPHED ARSENAL FOOTBALL
Donated by Alan Sunderland

2. AUTOGRAPHED BOXING GLOVE — HENRY COOPER & PAST CHAMPIONS
Donated by Frannie Peake

3. AUTOGRAPHED COPY OF ERIC CANTONA'S BIOGRAPHY
Donated by Dave Allard

4. FRAMED PHOTOGRAPH OF TERRY VENABLES
Signed to the purchasers requirements

Felixstowe F.C. wishes to acknowledge the invaluable support shown by tonights donators.

REMEMBER

The more tickets you buy the better your chance of winning these excellent raffle prizes.

Tonights programme is sponsored by Winsor Clarke Ltd, Print & Design, Pauls Road, Ipswich Telephone (0473) 254817

SPECIAL THANKS TO THE FOLLOWING FOR THEIR GENEROUS SUPPORT

Jobling and Knape Solicitors, Morecambe, Carnforth, Lancaster and Heysham

Lancaster Roofing Co., River Stree, St. George's Quay, Lancaster

Broombys Ltd., Euston Road, Morecambe

Hartley Plant Hire, Morecambe, Carnforth, Windermere and Barrow

British Gas North Western, Whitegate, Morecambe

M&H Hire, White Lund Ind. Est., Morecambe

Kitchen Design by Spencer, Unit 3, Northgate, White Lund, Morecambe

Granby Garments, White Lund, Morecambe

Heywood Glass, Ellesmere Road, Morecambe

Hodgson & Wrathall, 17 Princes Crescent, Bare, Morecambe

Lancaster Sawmills Ltd., Lune Ind. Est., Lancaster

Lancaster Pre-Cast Ltd., Lune Ind. Est., Lancaster

Auto Valeting Services, White Lund Estate, Morecambe

D&H Design, Hophouse Lane, Kirkby Lonsdale

Crewdson Fabrication Ltd., White Lund Trading Estate, Morecambe

Harbour & General Works Ltd., Morecambe
Mason's Carpets, Vickers Ind. Est., Morecambe

Adam and Gaskell Ltd., Lancaster, Morecambe and Carnforth

Clawsafe Scaffolding Ltd., White Lund, Morecambe

Kall-Kwik Printing, West Street, Morecambe

Cadel Limited, West Street, Morecambe,

Manhaven Limited, 5 Oakley Road, Morecambe, Crabtree Promain, 5 Oakley Road, Morecambe, Keystrokes, Sandylands House, Morecambe,

Bookers Cash & Carry, Morecambe

Sponsors

Sabden Football Club
extend thanks to the following for sponsorship

THE IMAGE WORKS LTD (Designers & Printers)

MATTHEW BROWN plc

TERRY CATTERMOLE (Timber Merchants)

SABDEN SERVICE STATION (A & M Ainsworth)

J & R WRIGHT (Builders) of Sabden

STIRK HOUSE HOTEL COUNTRY HOTEL, Gisburn

TERAL TISSUES LTD of Great Harwood

BRIAN DOOTSON (Peugeot) LTD of Clitheroe

WHITE HART INN of Sabden

J & S CROPPER (Family Butchers) of Sabden

PENDLE WITCH HOTEL of Sabden

JOHN JANEZCO PALLETS of Great Harwood

CELTECK LTD of Lancaster

INVICTA PAPERCRAFT LTD, Hythe, Kent

BARLOW ANDREWS of Bolton

FARNWORTH THOMMASON of Bolton

C. M. REPROGRAPHICS of Manchester

CLIVE KNIGHT COMMERCIALS of Sabden

S. G. ALUMINIUM LTD of Oswaldtwistle, Accrington

REIGILL (Civil Engineers) of Sabden

A.B.A. GENERAL INSURANCE LTD of Stockport

C. D. ELECTRONICS (Great Harwood) LTD of Simonstone, Burnley

C & J BARFORD (Newsagents) of Sabden

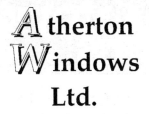

Part Three

INCOME

'If it's more than expenditure .... you're in profit'

11
The Raffle

The Raffle can be the largest fund-raiser of the evening. If it is organised well, it can attract between £5 and £10 per head. Here is how to make the most out of your raffle.

The Prizes

It is important to have a good selection of prizes on view at the function. A good position is on a table located to the right or left of the top table. The number of prizes should not exceed 12 to15, and the raffle should not take more than 10 to 15 minutes. Some organisations pride themselves on the quantity of their raffle prizes. They probably feel that more prizes = more chance of winning = more tickets sold. But rarely is this the case. A more probable equation is: more raffle prizes = guests get home later = no increase in revenue.

The prizes should include one large star prize, preferably a video, TV or music centre, which, displayed on top of its box, makes a good centrepiece for the others to be ranged around. A set of golf clubs with bag plus trolley always looks impressive.

Try not to spend too much money on raffle prizes. Ask each committee member, or each company table sponsor, to provide a prize (the company would then be mentioned during the evening when 'their' prize is drawn). If you cannot get someone to donate a star prize, then buy one at trade costing no more than £75-125, or get it in exchange for tickets to the event to the same value. When assembling prizes, do not forget to include a good selection of prizes for women, which your male guests can take home to their wives. A hair dryer, a set of women's golf clubs, a voucher for a couple of days at a health farm, etc, are always well received.

The SPORTSMAN's Dinner Business

£MT
Do not forget to ask the hotel for a raffle prize when you are 'just about' to book the function (a meal for two is a good prize).

Your Ticket-sellers

There is no doubt that the best method by far to sell tickets is by using attractive young ladies. This is not meant as a sexist remark, it is a simple fact based on statistics. Avoid asking the wives or daughters of committee members.

The perfect raffle girl is aged 20 to 30, attractively dressed, chatty, friendly and smiling – and is smart enough to understand that she is working. It is her job to complete the task as swiftly as possible at a time when every member of the table will want to chat to her and show off in front of his mates.

Although it can sometimes raise extra revenue, raffle girls who are topless or naked bring a very seedy element to the night, and for a quality event should be avoided.

The Tickets

Make sure you have enough books of tickets, and that each book is a different colour.

Some raffle tickets, of the cloakroom type, are difficult to tear and this can more than double the time it takes to go round the room. Check this in advance. You can also pre-tear tickets 1 to 4 (as a block) through a whole book, leaving the fifth ticket in place. This means the ticket-seller only needs to tear off one ticket when selling a strip of five, which speeds up the selling time enormously.

The Sales Pitch

Although the raffle is a crucial event, possibly the biggest fund-raiser of the night, some organisers do not give it enough thought. Raffle tickets are usually printed in strips of five. To get the most out of this, your Compere should encourage guests to buy tickets in strips, say at 5 for £5 and 15 for £10.* If he says, 'Tickets are £1.00 each,' this instantly plants the idea that it is possible to buy an individual ticket, and your total revenue would suffer.

Traditionally, 5 per cent of the attendance avoid buying raffle tickets. A well-timed visit to the toilet, a walk across to chat with a friend will be quietly planned to coincide with the raffle-seller approaching his table. An experienced raffle girl will joke about this with the rest of the table and leave a strip at his place, saying to the table, 'Tell him I'll be back, and I'll put my hand in his pocket even if he won't.'

'I once attended a dinner to raise money for a cricket club. There were over 250 guests. Raffle tickets were sold, as usual, at £5 for a strip of 5 and £10 for 15. Once the raffle-sellers had visited each table, the organiser instructed the Compere to announce, "We've only a few raffle tickets left. If anyone wants the last few they can have five strips, that's 25 tickets, for £10." Quite a few people took up this offer. Thus, tickets for this raffle were sold at three different prices: at £1 each (5 for £5), at 66.6p each (15 for £10), and finally at 40p each (25 for £10).

This meant that the final purchasers had a far better chance of winning than the early purchasers. This was obviously an unfair advantage but, as always, it seemed to be accepted by the audience who let the evening's fund-raising take its course.

The first Speaker (a famous jockey) had finished when the Compere announced the raffle draw. Just as the chairman of the club pulled out the first winning ticket, one of the audience stood up in the middle of the room and shouted, "Gentlemen, this is an illegal raffle, and I insist that it does not

* Under lottery laws it is not legal to sell tickets at different prices. However, at Sportsman's Dinners this is often overlooked as most guests accept that the proceeds are going to a charity or similar fund-raising organisation.

go ahead. I purchased my tickets at £1 each and other people have bought them for far less and it is unfair and illegal. I work for Customs & Excise and I am familiar with the law relating to lotteries like this and I insist that the draw stops immediately and all monies are refunded."

You could have cut the air with a knife. The organiser looked very embarrassed, and so did the club chairman, stuck up there on stage with a raffle ticket in his hand and his pants metaphorically around his ankles.

Life slowly returned to the audience and, amid the muttering, you could hear a few shouts of "Get on with it," "Don't listen to that stupid bugger," and also "Let's have our money back."

Luckily, the Compere was a professional and he handled the situation with great efficiency. He simply said: "Gentlemen, our friend is right, the raffle tickets were offered at different prices and that isn't exactly correct. But tonight we are here to raise money for DD Cricket Club and I assure you all profits are going to a good cause. If anyone wants to bring his tickets to the top table now we will pay £1 for each ticket. If you don't want your money back, shall we get on with the raffle? Let's have a show of hands if you agree with that."

As the night resumed its course, one very angry Customs & Excise official got his £5 back and left early. There was an extraordinary twist to the story when one of his tickets, which was still in the drum, was pulled out as a winner. It was decided that, as the club had effectively bought this ticket back, the item, a large bottle of Scotch, should be auctioned. It raised £25 and the money went to the club.'

IOT
**If you do offer tickets at different prices, do not push your
luck too far**

The Cash Element

The raffle is the main area in the evening where you have cash floating around, and you need to be careful. It is important to set up a system which is not seen as accusing anyone of being untrustworthy, but is organised well enough to reduce the chances of pilfering as much as possible. Remember, if tickets are sold at different prices, it is impossible to reconcile tickets sold with cash received.

It can easily happen that, when all the raffle tickets have been sold, a strange situation develops with piles of money, often thousands of pounds, being left around on tables, under tables, behind the raffle prizes, with the raffle-sellers, and so on. Someone could well feel tempted to dip into the treasure, and this is why you need a plan.

IOT
Decide what will happen to your raffle (and any other draw or auction) takings before the function begins!

The best way to handle raffle sales is as follows:
1   Sell your tickets at a fixed time, during the sweet course or coffee.
2   Make sure you have at least two ticket-sellers per 100 guests.
3   Issue each seller with a canvas bag (no handbags), a float of £5 for change, and a new book of raffle tickets (a different colour for each seller).
4   One committee member supervises each ticket-seller. The committee member tells the sellers which tables to cover and explains that, should any problems arise (running out of tickets, needing change, etc), he will be on hand to help. He keeps a watchful eye on the ticket-sellers until the Compere asks, 'Anyone not had raffle tickets? Please put up your hand.'

At this point the committee member walks to one of 'his' tables with his hand up, and stays there until the raffle sellers come over to him. Whether he buys any tickets is up to him, but it encourages sales generally if he can at least look like a potential buyer.

After a second announcement by the Compere – 'Anyone still not got raffle tickets?' – ticket-selling is concluded and the committee members and ticket-sellers walk out of the function room to a pre-arranged counting room. There they count the money together. A cash sheet is completed, the money is bagged in bank bags and the ticket-sellers are then paid. This payment can be deducted from the raffle figure on the cash sheet. The ticket-sellers and the committee members all sign the cash sheet, and the bag is then taken to the hotel safe, or some other secure place, for collection later. Under no circumstances should any individual be left alone with the money before it has been counted.

Payment for Entertainers

Some organisations prefer to pay their entertainers in cash from the proceeds of the raffle and other fund-raisers. If so, it is a good idea to separate this money and put it into envelopes as soon as the takings have been counted.

Have your treasurer prepare an envelope with the name of each entertainer and his fee written on the inside flap. The committee member in charge can then enter these monies on the cashing-up sheet.

IOT
**Never count money in the function room, and especially
never on the top table.**

12
The Draw

If organised well, the draw can become the second largest fund-raiser of the night, after the raffle. As a rule of thumb, the prize offered should be worth around 45 per cent of the gross takings. The general guidelines covering lotteries is that prizes must not be worth more than 50 per cent of the income. For example:

250 guests x £5 draw takings £1250
Top value of prize £600

100 guests x £5 draw takings £500
Top value of prize £200

200 guests x £10 draw takings £2000
Top value of prize £900

Looking at the equation in another way, do not announce a draw where 250 guests are asked to contribute £5, and the prize is a £10 bottle of Scotch.

£MT
Do not spend 45 per cent of the takings on buying a prize. Always look for sponsorship, a donation or a contra-deal.

There are certain key elements to every draw, as follows.

The Spend

A £10 or £20 draw will only be accepted without mutterings of complaint if the Compere states it is the ONLY fund-raiser of the night, or that it is being done for a very special reason. At most functions, if a £10 draw is attempted in conjunction with a raffle (and auction), it is likely to attract a negative response. However, a £5 draw plus raffle will be accepted because the majority of guests expect to spend around £25 on their evening out: £10-£15 on drinks, and £10-£15 on fund-raising.

The Prize

To attract a good response it is essential to offer a good prize. Some examples are:

*   Weekend for two in Paris/London plus show
*   Wembley weekend
*   Colour TV, music centre, video
*   Big-match tickets to football, rugby, tennis, golf, etc
*   Air tickets, hotel accommodation.

£MT
Never give cash as a prize. Even if a prize has to be
purchased, it is always possible to buy at a discount.

Timing

A good time to announce the draw is early in the evening. This keeps it well away from the raffle and does not ask guests to put their hands in their pockets on two occasions close together.

If the draw is announced during the soup course, the Compere can take the opportunity to welcome everyone, chat them through the night and then round off by saying, 'One of our fund-raisers this evening is a £? note draw. In front of you, you will find a brown envelope. Please place your £? note inside, write your name on the front and the girls will come amongst you and collect the envelopes. We have a wonderful prize this evening ....'

The Envelope

Use a C6 manila window envelope or a window wages envelope. Too often, 'for a laugh', guests place a piece of paper in the envelope and write someone else's name on it; a good joke, but costly for the organiser. The window envelope ensures that the banknote remains visible. This idea came out of Yorkshire – where else?

Change

Never attempt a £5 note draw unless you have laid in a sufficient stock of £5 notes as change. A good guide is to have 3 x £5 notes for every 2 people, eg 100 guests = £750 in £5 notes needed. The reason for this is simple. Less than 50 per cent of people carry £5 notes. If someone wants to change a £10 note, you need to give them 2 x £5 notes as change.

It is obviously essential to ensure that the money-collectors account for the change they give out by returning £10 notes equal to the float they were given in £5 notes.

£MT
Ensure that whoever collects the envelopes has a
collection bag (or money bag).

Making the Draw

The draw can be made early. It is a good opportunity to thank a Sponsor by acknowledging his company's sponsorship. Maybe they have provided the star prize free of charge or at cost. The draw for the winning prize can be done by the Sponsor, Celebrity Guest, Club Chairman, Guest of Honour, etc.

Once the draw has been completed, the bag containing all the envelopes should be sealed, stored safely, emptied and counted the following day, or counted immediately using the same routine as described in the previous section ('The Raffle'). The bag should also contain the change (£750, now in £10 notes), which goes back to the bank.

Business Card Draw

A simple Business Card Draw can sometimes deliver unexpected riches. Unknown to you, your club's next chairman, major investor, sponsor, next year's dinner sponsor, kit sponsor or table sponsor could be sitting there anonymously in the room. He could be a future Alan Sugar, Jack Walker, Max Griggs or Sir John Hall ... just wanting to be asked.

If he does not have a business card on him, even this draw will not identify him, but it is certainly worth a try. The draw is always worth the cost of the prize. It works like this:

Compere: 'Gentlemen, while you are dining, the beautiful Raquel will be moving around the room asking you to put your business card in the champagne bucket for our FREE Business Card Draw.

'As soon as Raquel has been round all the tables, I will ask Mr Dougie Doings, tonight's Guest of Honour, to select one card and the winner will have a bottle of iced champagne delivered immediately to his table. Raquel will pour.'

Even if there is only a 20-30 per cent take-up, who knows, Jack Walker's business card could be in there. In any event, you can add every new name to your database for mailing out before next year's dinner.

13
Stand-Up Bingo

Stand-Up Bingo, or Ognib (Bingo backwards) or Irish Bingo, has been very popular for many years. It can replace either the raffle or the lucky draw or, if around £10 is charged (for two, three or four games), it can replace both of these fund-raisers and become the only fund-raiser for the night.

The key attraction, which puts it above draws or raffles, is the 'audience participation' element. Unlike a draw or raffle, where only the winners stand up in front of an audience, in Stand-Up Bingo the last 20, then 12, then 8 etc participants stand up in front of the audience and this creates a good atmosphere. From a cash point of view it can eliminate the dodger (the guest who leaves the room for the toilet once the raffle ticket-sellers get near them), as everyone with a ticket stands up to play. The ones who are sitting down have obviously not bought a ticket, which causes them some embarrassment.

The basic principles of the game are this:

1   Everyone buys a bingo ticket (or two if they wish)
2   Everyone with a ticket stands up
3   The Compere calls out numbers from 1 to 90
4   If a number is called that is on a guest's ticket, he sits down
5   The last person standing up is the winner.

The game is easy to administer, inexpensive to organise and it is possible to run two or three games using the same ticket, or have a different-coloured ticket for each game.

Tickets are sold in the same manner as raffle tickets, or can be left at each place setting when the tables are being set. The ticket sellers simply go round and collect the money.

Once again, good prizes are important. If tickets are sold during the soup course, this will ensure a take-up of over 95 per cent as early in the evening very few people will leave the table to visit the toilet.

£MT
Never give cash as a prize.

Stand-Up Bingo can be administered either with a computerised selector, an automatic Bingo machine using ping-pong balls or similar, by pulling numbers out of a bag, or by listing numbers on a plain piece of paper. The Compere simply crosses out any number at random.

Alternatively, if you buy bingo tickets in books of five, the first five tickets in the book contain all ninety numbers (didn't know that, did you?) So these five tickets can be used to call out numbers and cross them off.

IOT
Use the first five Bingo tickets to call the numbers.

Just in case your electrical gadgets do not work, or somebody stands on a numbered ping-pong ball or you have bought your Bingo tickets individually and not in strips, on the next page is a prepared sheet of numbers for you. If you want to use it for more than one game, use a cross to mark the numbers for the first game and circles for the second, etc.

As the game is sometimes called Irish Bingo, I will remind you simply to photocopy the page, and then you can use it again and again. (This will save you a lot of money on Tippex!)

1	2	3	4	5	6	7	8	9	10
11	12	13	14	15	16	17	18	19	20
21	22	23	24	25	26	27	28	29	30
31	32	33	34	35	36	37	38	39	40
41	42	43	44	45	46	47	48	49	50
51	52	53	54	55	56	57	58	59	60
61	62	63	64	65	66	67	68	69	70
71	72	73	74	75	76	77	78	79	80
81	82	83	84	85	86	87	88	89	90

Simply cross off the numbers at random. Use a different mark, eg cross, circle, underline for each game.

If you are calling the numbers, do not forget to add a bit of life to the game even if it kills you! Remember, it's: Kelly's Eye, No 1; Legs Eleven; Unlucky for some, No 13; Blind 20; All the Threes, 33; How I like 'em, 17; How I get 'em, 72; Heinz, 57; Clickety Click, 66; Six and Nine, 69, 'a lot go down on that one'; Two Fat Ladies, 88; Top of the Shop, 90. We have heard it all before, but the game sounds very drab if the numbers are simply called out individually, for example: 'The first number is sixty-four; next twenty-three; next fifty-five, next .... ZZZZZZZZZ!

Good Meal, Brilliant Speaker, Great Beer

.........WHAT A NIGHT!

At John Smith's Ltd, we're great supporters of Sportsman's Dinners and are confident our team of brands, including John Smith's Bitter, Theakston's Best Bitter, Fosters, Kronenbourg 1664, Miller, Beck's and Holsten will make your evening a great success.

To help with fundraising, we are pleased to be able to offer you a unique idea to save you money on bingo tickets.

A DISTINCTIVE FULL-FLAVOURED BITTER, BREWED AT THE TADCASTER BREWERY YORKSHIRE.

Simply complete the form below to claim your free stand-up bingo beer mats. We will send you by return of post, the quantity you require (up to 500 maximum).

It would be worthwhile photocopying this page in case you wish to order again.

Name . . . .

Address . . . .

. . . .

. . . .

Postcode . . . .

Tel . . . .

Please send . . . . Beer Mat BingoTickets
(Actual Size:- 3.5" x 3.5")

STAND UP BINGO

Rules of the Game

1. Everyone playing stands up
2. If a number is called on your ticket, sit down
3. The last one standing is the winner

3	11		30		51			70	82
	14	21		46	57	63			
7		22	39	48		68	74	90	

The winning ticket will be checked
after the game

Return to: The Marketing Department, John Smith's Ltd, The Brewery, Tadcaster, North Yorkshire, LS24 9SA

Heads or Tails

This game is basically an extension or derivative of Stand-Up Bingo, without the need to use a ticket to play. The basic rules are as follows:

1   Everyone pays to play.
2   Everyone stands up.
3   Everyone selects either heads or tails by putting both their hands on their head or bottom (tails).
4   The Compere or guest tosses a coin. If it lands on heads, everyone with their hand on their tails sits down.
5   Everyone still on his feet then chooses again, either heads or tails.
6   Through this process of elimination, the last person left standing is the winner.

This game is quick, simple and fun. To collect money, just ask each table to put a £1 coin (or £2, £5 or £10) into a glass at the centre of the table.

IOT
Collect the money before the game starts. It is hard to
collect money from people who have just lost.

For a bit of variety, this game can also be played by selecting which one of two cards (the size of playing cards) to raise, rather than putting hands on heads or tails. Prior to the function a red and a yellow card is left by each place setting. The Compere tosses a coin in the usual way.

HEADS means [RED (sent off)]   TAILS means [YELLOW (booked)]

£MT
Get the cards sponsored by selling an advertisement on
the reverse of the card. A taxi company is a good
prospect.

Kings and Queens

This is exactly the same as Heads or Tails except the audience are asked to be either Kings (by putting their hands on their heads as a crown) or Queens (when they stand with their hands on their hips in an effeminate pose). Heads is Kings, Tails is Queens.

To Collect Money

As well as putting a glass on the table, you can also nominate a table representative. For example, your Compere announces: 'To collect the money on your table, would you all now point to the most handsome (ugliest, fattest, richest, tightest, most educated) member of your table. Could he now collect the money from the other more beautiful (uglier, thinner, poorer – opposite of first adjective) guests.'

This usually gets a laugh and soon produces table representatives to collect the money.

14
The Auction

If the mood of the evening is good, the auction can be the biggest fund-raiser of the night. Usually it is rated as the third largest fund-raiser, after the raffle and the draw. A notable exception to this is the evening specifically billed as a 'Fund-raising Auction', such as Children In Need evenings. I once attended a function in Wakefield organised by Empire Stores where over £24,000 was raised for charity by auctioning off over 50 items. At a football testimonial dinner in Aberdeen, over £7,000 was raised from 10 auction items – an incredible return.

A good auction has three key ingredients:

1   Quality auction items (3-5 maximum)
2   A good auctioneer
3   Rich guests prepared to bid. (In Aberdeen, the farmers and the oilmen always want to outdo each other.)

Many other secondary ingredients add to the success of the auction. These include the atmosphere, a good meal, Speakers and a Comedian who perform well, a clear PA system, choosing the right time (before midnight is a must), and rival tables.

Traditionally, the auction comes at the end of the event, but it is not uncommon to auction one or two items either in between Speakers or before the Comedian. The concept of the auction is simple: good food plus lots of drink plus good entertainment equals bidders who will (for their own reasons) pay above the odds. They want to play their part in the entertainment and this is their opportunity to be noticed. Some also enjoy the opportunity to let everyone in the room know that they are rich.

Auction Items

There are some tried and tested auction items that will always raise from £75 to £150. They include autographed balls (football, rugby) and cricket bats; autographed shirts (football, cricket or rugby); an autographed team or individual photograph or painting, and air tickets. Other tried and tested items, which usually raise much more money, are international shirts, international caps and, on the rare occasions they come up, Cup and League winners' medals plus a miscellany of similar items: the snooker cue that won the world title, the running shoes that won the gold medal, the tennis racket that ... and so on.

Other ideas that have been used include:

*   **Tickets to an Event or Show plus Overnight Accommodation**
    These are always popular because they have an easily perceived value of around £150 to £250 and anyone buying the tickets can go home and tell his wife he has won them at the function. (This makes it easier for him to go to the next 'night out with the boys'.)

*   **A Cup Final Weekend**
    Although it is illegal to auction or raffle match tickets, some organisers purchase a corporate hospitality package, which includes overnight accommodation and can be legitimately auctioned.

*   **Limited Edition Prints or Photographs**
    These are especially treasured if the celebrity guest can personally sign the print or photograph. The key to this auction item is undoubtedly the frame. A quality 2-3in mahogany frame with a gilt inner slip and 2-3in mount will make the item look expensive. On the other hand, a 1in frame without mount will make it look cheap.

£MT
The framed print should have plain glass (not non-reflective). When held high to the lights this will reflect around the room, making the print look expensive. This simple tip will add a few pounds to the perceived value of the item.

* **Big-match Tickets**
  A pair of tickets (either with or without accommodation) to a major sporting event, eg Wimbledon, The Oval, St Andrews, The Crucible, The Grand National, British Grand Prix, etc. It must be stressed that many tickets cannot be resold at above face value. In these examples the tickets are included at face value, with the event 'package' being offered for auction.

* **Mystery Prize**
  This is a really risky idea. If the prize is two Club World tickets to LA and it sells for £100, it is a mistake. At the other end of the scale, if it is two tickets for Des O'Connor in Bournemouth, and it sells for £1000, it is an even bigger mistake.

* **Use of a Car**
  For a weekend, or a week. This is easy to get sponsored and a good opportunity for a local garage to have a new vehicle test-driven. The highest bidder is usually someone with sufficient funds to purchase the car.

There is one essential role at every auction. Someone must take responsibility to note WHO made the final bid and HOW MUCH they bid. Although this sounds straightforward, at the end of a frantic evening it is easy to let the auction take its course, without taking careful note of who the bidders were.

It is also advisable to make immediate contact with the successful bidders, once the auction is concluded, to find out how they intend to pay. Obviously, if it is the chairman's brother or the club captain who have purchased the items, it can be sorted out the next day, unless of course they are traditionally bad payers.

If the winning bidders have been invited as guests and are strangers to your club or organisation, it is a good idea to get a business card or telephone number, or better still a cheque. If they have had a good evening at your dinner, they may take a table next year. Add them to your contact list.

The example quoted in the Introduction to this book indicates how costly it can be when the organisers do not concentrate their minds at an auction.

£MT
Make sure somebody is responsible for identifying the successful bidders, noting how much they bid and collecting the money.

15
Other Fund-raisers

As we have seen, there are four main fund-raisers: the Raffle, the Draw, the Auction and Stand-up Bingo. Here are some other activities which can be used in place of or in addition to these basic ones.

Select a Team

In this simple game, each guest is asked to select his best team from the selection offered on the entry sheet. He can have one entry, or more if he wishes to spend more money. The Celebrity Guest is then asked to select his team, which becomes the winning side. Any guest who selects the same team as the Celebrity Guest wins a prize. If no-one has exactly the same team, the winner is the entry with the highest number of players appearing in the Celebrity's team.

Use entry-sheets with a tear-off strip on which guests can write a copy of their answers before the main sheet is collected to be checked. Other quicker ways to check the sheets are to trust the guest to check his own sheet, or exchange sheets with his neighbour.

A selection of teams appears at the back of this book in Appendix I: Competitions. These can be used for your function or you can produce your own, especially if another sport would be more appropriate to your club or your Speaker.

No particular skill is required from your guests. To ensure the game is more of a lottery than a game of skill, ask your Celebrity to include one odd or unexpected choice.

Recommendation *This is an excellent game, easy to administer and a lot of fun.*

The Quiz

The Quiz can sometimes cause a problem. If it is too easy, nearly everybody wins; if it is too hard, guests tend to share the answers with each other and again there can be too many winners. But quizzes are popular and people like to answer sporting questions.

Whoever composes the quiz also has to ensure that the answers are exactly right. There must be no ambiguities or incorrect answers. There is always one bright spark who will want to show off his depth of knowledge to the audience by questioning the correctness of an answer. If there is a good prize at stake, he will try even harder. For example:

Question: Who was England's first black international?
Answer (according to the quiz book) : Viv Anderson.

But I have heard this answer questioned on a number of occasions. It is also ambiguous as it could refer to a cricket, rugby, tennis or boxing international.

IOT
**Trivial Pursuit or quiz books can provide suitable
questions for a good quiz.**

Alternatively, there is always the 'Lottery Quiz'. Here the questions are so difficult that no-one can be expected to know the answers. Players choose from one of three answers, and most of the time have to guess. The questions must be valid but they need to be very obscure or out of the way.

For example:
Question: When hit or kicked, which travels the fastest? A baseball, golf ball, tennis ball, cricket ball, or ice hockey puck?
Answer: Tennis ball. Greg Rusedski's serve was measured at 149mph in March 1998. The other balls travel at between 85mph (golf ball) and 95mph (football).

IOT
The Guinness Book of Records is always a good reference source for this type of question.

Recommendation *It is better to use a game of chance than a game of intelligence or knowledge. See '101 Great Sporting Questions' (with answers) in Appendix I.*

The Picture Quiz

The idea behind quizzes and questions is simply to get guests talking, joking and networking around the table. To this end, the Picture Quiz works very well. It is simple to prepare and works best if you mix a few well-known faces with a few obscure ones.

A couple of newspapers, supplements or sports magazines will be sufficient to provide 10, 20 or 30 faces for your audience to identify. Do not forget to leave a space below the face for the answer. And make sure to number each face to save confusion when the answers are read out. An example of this type of quiz can be found at the end of this book (see 'Guess the Face' in Appendix I).

Recommendation *This is easy to prepare and good fun. For an extra laugh, try to include a childhood photo of your guest Speaker or Chairman.*

The Logo Quiz

A more serious variant of the Picture Quiz is the Logo Quiz, the rules of which are self-explanatory. Many well-known logos are scattered around newspapers and magazines. Although most are recognisable, it is amazing how hard it is to remember which company the logo represents. There is a sample quiz in Appendix I at the end of this book.

Recommendation *This can be very interesting, a real brain-teaser.*

The Dutch Auction

The Dutch Auction works like this. The Compere announces that 'numbers' will cost £1 (or £5, £10 or £20). Guests choose a number and shout it out. They then put their stake into a barrel (box, hat, bag or something similar) which is passed around the room. Guests can have more than one entry, but they must remember their numbers. As proof, ask them to write down each number on a piece of paper which they place on the table in front of them until the winning number is announced.

When the game starts, someone shouts out 'ONE' (he puts £1 into the barrel), another guest shouts 'TWO' (he puts his £1 into the barrel), then 'THREE' ... 'FOUR' ... 'FIFTY' ... 'EIGHTY', etc.

The amount of entries is usually governed by the value of the prize on offer. For example, a gallon of whisky should be worth about 100 entries at £1 each. Two Club World tickets on BA to Barbados may encourage 500 entries at £5 each.

The winning number can either be preselected and placed in a sealed envelope, or selected at random on the night.

Recommendation *This game can be hard work but it creates audience participation. The only drawback is that it can take too long.*

The Alternative Auction

In most towns and cities there is a great rivalry between two sporting teams. For example, in Manchester both supporters of Manchester United and Manchester City feel their team to be superior, and hate to see the rival team win. At a Sportsman's Football Dinner in Manchester, should there be one United and one City autographed football to auction, the supporters of whichever team's ball is auctioned second will invariably ensure it goes for a higher price than the first ball. So, whatever price the first ball brings sets the standard for the second ball, eg Man United £150, Man City £160, or vice versa.

In the Alternative Auction, both balls are offered simultaneously, with bids being encouraged for either ball. In this version, the rival fans usually push the prices, and each other, beyond the levels you would expect with a single ball. To make an Alternative Auction work, you need two items from two rival teams, two sets of supporters present in the audience, a good Compere or auctioneer (as always), a good atmosphere in the room and, finally, as said many times before, a good PA system.

I have seen so many fabulous auction prizes go under the hammer for hundreds of pounds below their potential value all because the venue did not have a good microphone system. For an investment of about £25, this could bring in hundreds of pounds more and also improve the quality of the evening.

Recommendation *A very good fund-raiser, if it is appropriate.*

£MT
A good PA system is essential.

Spot the Ball

This game is pretty straightforward, though a little costly and messy to prepare. Like the newspaper version, the main element is a large action photograph (usually of a football match, though it can be done with golf, rugby or cricket) with the ball missing from the shot. The guests are sold pins, each marked with a number, and the guest's name is written in a book next to his number. He buys one pin for £5, three pins for £10, etc, and then walks to the large photograph and puts his numbered pin or pins where he thinks the ball should be.

Once each pin has been placed on the picture, the Celebrity or Chairman is given the original photograph showing the location of the ball. He then goes up to the picture and selects which number is the nearest. This becomes the winning entry.

There are some drawbacks:

1   The picture enlargement can be costly (5ft x 4ft can be around £150-£200). A cheaper version is a multi-picture enlargement, costing around £50, which is done by blowing up sections of a 10in x 8in photograph on a colour copier. Each section is copied onto A3 (approx 17in x 12in) and is then pieced together with the others. If a 'spray mount' is used, you cannot see the joins from 4-5ft away.

2   The photograph or sectioned copy needs to be mounted on a pinboard or piece of foam board, otherwise it will not be easy to place the pins. This board (5ft x4ft) should cost around £25.

3   The pins need to be individually numbered or have a flag-type number attached. This can be a time-consuming job.

4   An easel or firm fixing to a wall is required. If the picture falls down and some of the pins come out, throw yourself off the top of the hotel!

5   Even though you have the original photograph, there may still be disagreement over where the ball should be, especially if the prize is a good one. The game may seem like just a bit of fun, but you always get one who knows better: 'I was at that match,' he says, 'and I don't remember the ball being there ....'

Recommendation *A novel fund-raiser, but costly and risky.*

Stand Up Bing ......O...... No!

Some organisations try their own version of Stand Up Bingo. It goes something like this. Everyone is sold a raffle ticket (cloakroom type) starting at number one, or they can buy three or four if they wish. Then numbers are drawn from a hat or drum right up until the last person is standing.

Question: What happens if all the numbers are called and there are still 10 people left standing?

Answer: You start all over again (with 10 unhappy people who know one of them has just missed out on a prize).

This game rarely works well as some people are often out at the toilet, on the telephone, etc, etc. Some do not hear their numbers called. Even though checks can be made as to which numbers were called, it is still messy.

Recommendation *Definitely NO!*

The Table Draw

A free draw can be a great start to the evening. Immediately after Grace, the Compere announces:

'Gentlemen, please remain upstanding at your tables. In the hat in front of me I have the 15 numbers of the 15 tables. If I draw your table number will you please sit down. The first table number is ...' and so on, until: 'The last table standing have just won half a dozen bottles of wine sponsored by DD Wine Importers – the best place in town for all your wine requirements. Gentlemen, please enjoy the wine and I hope we all have a great evening.'

As I said, it is a great start to the night, 'A free draw,' think the guests, 'a winning table, six bottles of wine (worth £60?), no mention of buying a raffle ticket. It's going to be a great night, let's have a another drink.'

Recommendation *If you can find a wine sponsor, go for it!*

The Big, Brown Envelope

Many organisations prefer to use this method to sell all the evening's fund-raisers in one hit. It works like this, beginning with the Compere's announcement:

'Gentlemen, in front of you in the centre of the table you will find a big brown envelope, and in it you will find 10 bingo tickets, 10 pick-your-team entries and 10 sets of raffle tickets. These are the only fund-raisers we will be having this evening, so can I ask each of you to put a £5 (or £10 or £20, depending on the audience) note in the brown envelope in exchange for entry to these competitions. Can I also ask one table member to nominate himself as captain and ensure that each guest on the table puts in to enter the fund-raisers. Shortly (or during the evening) the girls (or committee members) will be coming round the tables to collect the envelopes.'

The advantages of this system are:

1   The girls (or committee members, you will probably not need pretty girls to encourage sales as each guest pays the same amount to enter the competitions) only go to each table once, and only need to deal with the captain of that table to collect the big, brown envelope.

2   It is easy to forecast your revenue. Base your projections on 95 per cent of the attendance putting in the amount the Compere requests.

3   Your guests only have to put their hands in their pockets once.

Disadvantages:

1   On each table of 7,8,9,10 people, some raffle tickets get left in the envelopes. It is virtually impossible to check which these are against which tickets go into the drum; consequently, these unsold tickets may be pulled out as winning tickets when the raffle is drawn.

2   This system does not give the 'big hitter' the chance to buy £10, £20 or £50 worth of raffle tickets to impress his colleagues (and there is always one).

3   The table captain (who may be the table sponsor or a host) could be embarrassed to ask for money from guests he has himself invited and

paid for. Some table sponsors feel obliged to pay for their guests' share in the contents of the big brown envelope.

4   Some guests, or even tables, take out the tickets and do not put money in. If the envelope is sealed, this may not be noticed until the envelope is opened later. If one person has not put money in, there is little you can do without causing embarrassment. If the whole table has not put in, it is worth going back to the table to point this out.

IOT
**Always put table numbers on the big brown envelopes
and check the contents before any of the games begin.**

Recommendation *Although it is a convenient way to raise funds, you are putting all your eggs in one basket. Be careful.*

Artist's Drawings

One tried and tested method of raising additional funds at sporting dinners is via the limited-edition drawing (or caricature) of your Celebrity Guest. The work can be based on an existing photograph. Although only the original is autographed and auctioned on the night of the dinner, a few extra copies can be reserved for your special guests.

To make a real impact, a caricature of the Celebrity Guest shaking hands with the main Sponsor is also a good investment, and this too can be done from photographs. David Foster from Ainsdale, near Southport (tel 01704 576032) is a particularly talented artist who excels at this sort of work, which has been used in various ways to raise funds.

Recommendation *This is an excellent fund-raiser if you are looking for something a little different.*

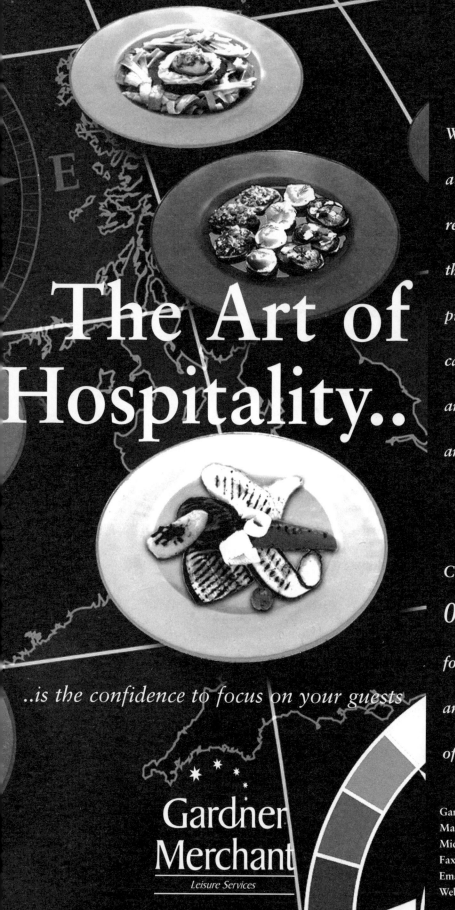

16
Sponsorship

The concept of sponsorship is quite a simple one. It is a method of creating either additional business or brand-name awareness by linking a company name (or in some cases the company product or service) to an event, in exchange for a fee.

If a company links its name to a Sportsman's Dinner, there are various ways to ensure that everyone who attends the event is aware of this sponsorship.

For example:

* Through mention in the sales letter announcing the function
* Using the ticket (front or reverse) to carry the Sponsor's advertisement
* Advertising the event in a newspaper, on radio or TV
* Using the menu (an advertisement could appear here also)
* Promoting the event with posters
* On arrival: placing banners on the car park entrance
* The table plan: another important opportunity that everyone sees
* Hotel Welcome board
* Place card (if Sponsor's name and telephone number is included, guests may keep it)
* Below the first-course plate. If a Sponsor's business card is placed there beforehand, it is revealed when the waitress takes away the plate.
* Chairs: place a Sponsor's brochure on each dining chair
* Place setting: an opportunity for product sampling or a free offer
* Behind top table: posters, banners, advertising boards, etc
* In the room: exhibition stand, product sampling, display of product
* By Compere: acknowledgment or welcome

* Raffle, draw or auction prize donations: acknowledgments to Sponsor
* Chairman's thank-you
* Press photograph: always ensure Sponsors are photographed with the Celebrity Speaker

IOT

Refuse any photographs of celebrities unless the photographer allows your Sponsors to be included in the photograph. This will ensure that if the newspaper publishes a photograph, your Sponsors will be featured. Do not compromise with photographers. You are in charge. Tell the photographer exactly what you require.

* Thank-you letter after event: another opportunity to acknowledge Sponsor
* Raffle-ticket girls: T-shirts with Sponsor's logo
* Serviettes, napkins, matches, etc
* Promotional give-away at table: pen, golf ball, diary, etc.

In addition to these 22 examples, there must be many more which can be individually tailored to ensure your Sponsor gets adequate coverage on the night.

To demonstrate the value of a sponsorship package, offer the menu of opportunities listed above to the Sponsor, each with a price. A reasonable yardstick is to mark up your costs by 100 per cent. Below is a straightforward sponsorship proposal showing your costs and your profit.

Sponsorship Package

	Value to Sponsor	Cost to You
Two tables of 10 (£350)*	700	700
5 bottles of wine per table	150	100
VIP reception	150	100
2 seats on top table @ £35*	70	70
Acknowledgment on tickets	50	–
Acknowledgment on menu	100	–
Celebrity photograph	100	–
Poster-brochure placements	100	–
Total	1420	970

* Ticket prices are shown at full sale price. Should the sponsorship not be sold, you would expect those tables or tickets to be sold at full price (see also separate section on Corporate Entertainment).

Sale price of sponsorship	2000
Perceived value	1420
Cost of sponsorship	970
Profit on sponsorship	£1030

As an added incentive you can also offer your Sponsor additional tickets or tables at cost price (provided the evening will not be a sell-out and there is plenty of room to add a few more tables).

If tickets are £35.00 each and the meal costs you £12.50, do not be scared to offer your Sponsor an extra couple of tables (to the rear of the room) for staff or special employees at £17.50 per head or £150 for a table of 10 (a saving of £200 per table). This is a great bargain for the Sponsor and makes added profit for you. Provided your price covers the cost of the meal, the secondary spend of these extra guests on raffles, draws and auctions is a further bonus for you. Who knows, if they enjoy the night, next year they may pay the full price to attend.

Only make this offer to your Sponsor and nobody else. You will make a lot of enemies if tickets are sold at different prices to standard guests.

There are many different ways of calculating how much profit you require from sponsorship. For a Sportsman's Dinner, sponsorship could be sold for £5 or £10,000 depending on the event. But if your Sponsor gets value for money, is happy that guests enjoyed the evening, is satisfied that his company name or product received adequate acknowledgment and feels that somewhere in the future there will be additional business, he has had a good deal.

The figures shown above are very basic, and organisers are free to charge any amount that a Sponsor is prepared to pay. However, it is important to leave the Sponsor happy with the deal. Then you can approach him again for your next dinner.

£MT
If you feel your Sponsor was happy with the event, the best time to ask him to sponsor your next event is THE VERY NEXT DAY. Strike while the iron is hot. Ring him to thank him and remember to ask if he will sponsor next time. Then write and confirm.

Table Sponsors

Apart from the main sponsorship, there are also some smaller sponsorship packages to be considered. The second most popular sponsorship package is table sponsorship. For example, at an event where individual tickets are £30 per head, a table sponsorship could be sold at £400 or £500 for a table of 10. The package could include:

* Acknowledgment or advertisement on menu
* Free champagne draw
* Free wine for table sponsors
* Compere to introduce table sponsors.

Indeed, some functions are only sold on the basis of table sponsorship. It must not be overlooked that this type of sponsorship can be invoiced directly to the company and some element can be claimed as genuine business expenditure. From a sales point of view, sponsored tables are efficient because you only need to complete 25 successful sales to fill a sporting dinner of 250 people on tables of 10 people. On the other hand, if tickets are sold on an individual basis, over a hundred sales transactions may be necessary as tickets will be sold in groups of 2, 3 or 4.

Point To Ponder

Another important consideration is the corporate entertainment aspect. If tables are sold on this basis, the guest invited by the Sponsor and indeed the Sponsor himself come to the dinner free of charge. Often the wine, hotel rooms, cigars, etc, are added to the company's bill. This will form part of the company's entertainment budget and is a legitimate business expense.

It then follows that these invited guests will contribute far more readily to the draws, raffles or auction because they know that eventually this 'free night out' will only cost them the price of a few fund-raising tickets. On occasion, some 'macho' guests (often fired up by wine) may even try to impress their host by going way over the top when purchasing raffle tickets or making outrageous bids to secure an auction prize.

How to Sell Sponsorship

If you are looking to sell sponsorship for the first time, are new to selling, and are wondering how to go about it, I have no easy solutions (Rule No 1, there are no rules!). The first things you need are a positive attitude, and lots of determination. If handled correctly, sponsorship can be very rewarding for both sponsor and the recipient. That is something you should always bear in mind. Meanwhile, here are a few dos and don'ts that may be helpful.

There are probably only 5 sales methods:

1   The friendly sale
2   The blunderbuss technique
3   The direct target
4   The cold call
5   Advertising.

To explain in more detail:

1   The Friendly Sale
The friendly sale is the place to start. Once you have worked out your sponsorship prices and prepared a package to offer to a potential sponsor, start with a 'friendly' target. Some friendly companies could be owned by:

*   Friends, neighbours or relations
*   Team members or family and friends of team members
*   Suppliers of kit, food, medical equipment, grass seed, etc
*   Brewery – most breweries are keen sponsors but are asked to sponsor more than most other companies
*   Local pub, disco, nightclub or restaurant.

All the above will have some vested interest in the organisation they are asked to sponsor. Without doubt this list provides the most potential. Do not move on to the other options until you have exhausted all your friendly ones.

2   The Blunderbuss Technique
This technique is used extensively in sales or marketing and usually centres on the traditional 'mailshot'. To help you with this, there is a standard letter on the next page which you can use. You send these to

companies listed in the Yellow Pages, Thompson Directory, Chamber of Commerce list, etc, or a list purchased from a marketing company.

Try to make your letter different. Make it stand out from the rest of the morning mail, make it colourful, cheeky, humorous or classy. Try to give the recipient a flavour of your function in the letter you send.

The response to such mailshots is usually around 2 per cent if you are lucky, but it does not follow that you only need to mail 100 companies to get two sponsors. Here are a few tips to increase the potential of your sponsorship letters:

* Always address the letter to a person. Do not send it to the 'Marketing Manager' or 'Sales Manager' but to the person by name. Ninety-eight out of a hundred of them will throw it in the bin. But they will think more favourably of you, as they screw up your letter, if you have addressed it to them personally. And never send a sponsorship proposal to 'Dear Sir'. This could hit the bin before the first paragraph is read.

* Follow up with a phone call. Ask for Mr Doings by name. No matter how many meetings he is in, keep ringing until you can speak to him personally and explain the sponsorship benefits.

* If you include a tear-off strip to your letter, always attach a pre-addressed or reply-paid envelope.

* Try to 'mail merge' your letter as shown in the example that follows. By personalising a letter in this way, you make your potential Sponsor feel his company is being asked individually rather than by mass mail. Most standard PCs have this facility.

* Think of how the sponsorship will benefit his company and have a few examples ready if you get to meet him. If you cannot think of any benefits, do not try to sell sponsorship to that company. Look for the 'edge'.

* Do not approach any multi-national companies unless you have a contact there which brings them into the friendly category. Your letter will simply hit the bin with the other seven or eight sponsorship letters they received that morning.

Checklist

If you sell table sponsorship, here is a good planning strategy that will work for your table sponsor. Suggest that he:

a) Lists 12 guests he would like to invite.

1) Himself	Tel	9)	Tel
2)	Tel	10)	Tel
3)	Tel	11)	Tel
4)	Tel	12)	Tel
5)	Tel	13)	Tel
6)	Tel	14)	Tel
7)	Tel	15)	Tel
8)	Tel	16)	Tel

b) Adds four reserves just in case.

c) Rings them personally to invite them (he will have far more success this way than asking his secretary to ring, or sending a written invitation). Allow two days to complete the task.

d) Writes confirming their attendance and saying that he will forward the tickets and detailed arrangements nearer to the function date.

He should remember that this is a planned corporate entertainment strategy intended to create more business for his company, and any additional attention to detail will be welcomed by his guests.

Sample Mailing Letter

date

Mr Dougie Doings
Company Name
Address and
postcode

Dear Mr Doings,

Stop.

Stop what you are doing, switch off your phone, leave the other unopened letters on your desk and read these few words.

When was the last time you socialised with your most precious clients, customers or colleagues? No, not out on a business lunch, but somewhere else just simply talking about everything except the business between you both.

Incredibly, it is now understood that this type of meeting and communicating can bring you more business success than most other sales and marketing techniques put together. Do you know that some companies spend 90% of their marketing budget this way. Many years ago this percentage was spent on advertising for new customers.

There are people out there who you need to get to know better; more importantly, they need to get to know you better!

That said, here's an idea that could be of interest to achieve this aim. Sponsor a table at the DD Cricket Club annual dinner. Guest Speaker, Dougie Doings, ex-England wicket-keeper and now TV commentator; Comedian, Dougie Doings, recently on TV, and Compere the inimitable Dougie Doings. It's going to be a great night. Your clients and customers will love it. I've also included a checklist that you might find helpful.

Yours sincerely,

Dougie (Use a blue ink pen to sign)

Dougie Doings

PS Don't forget to switch your phone back on. Have a great day.

IOT
Always sign the letter personally, preferably in blue ink.
Black ink could suggest your signature is photocopied.
Make sure the address label is attached to the envelope
perfectly straight and central; the stamp should also be
straight and in the top right-hand corner. Also, never send
a mailshot in brown manila envelopes. This advice will
not persuade the Marketing Manager to sponsor your
event, but such attention to detail will show that you
care about presentation and that you may therefore take
care when looking after the Sponsor's interest.

'In my office I have adopted a system where, if a mailshot (they are easy to detect from the real mail) has my name, company name or address spelt incorrectly, or if the label has been 'slapped' on and is not straight, I simply throw it straight in the bin without opening it. If a sales company does not take the trouble to mail me correctly, I do not take the trouble to open the envelope.'

3   The Direct Target

This method takes the most time but can pay the highest dividends. Use a bit of lateral thinking when you consider which type of company you are going to approach. Here are some examples:

*   If your function is the type that will attract a lot of young people, a bank may see this as an opportunity to open new accounts. Maybe a joint promotion can take place on the night. For example, for all new accounts opened within seven days of the dinner, the club gets an additional bonus.

*   If your function will attract Captains of Industry – managers, directors, sales managers, etc – motor companies could be an ideal sponsor. This type of introductory meeting could be worth a fleet of cars to the right garage. A Business Card Draw on the night could offer lots of leads.

*   If your function will attract only local people, as would a village football team, local golf club, cricket club, etc, look for a new

company that has just moved into the area. It does not have to be an ICI or a Sainsbury's. Think of the new Exhaust Centre, Double Glazing Company, MOT Centre, even a shop or restaurant. If they are to be successful, the people running these new businesses need to get to know the community. Supporting a local club via sponsorship is seen as an excellent gesture and will certainly receive support from all attending the function.

* Look also for the small company just starting to grow. They may be a company that would not usually be asked to sponsor, but now their sponsorship would be a method of announcing that their company has arrived in a bigger league. These companies can often be found in the local newspaper or by listening to the local radio station. Do not forget, it is not a McDonalds or Marks & Spencer you are looking for, more a DD Investments or DD Landscape Gardeners or DD Restaurant.

4   The Cold Call

Without doubt, cold calling is the most difficult, deflating form of selling known to man. Be ready to be rejected on a regular basis. People will be rude to you, refuse to see you, ignore you, even kick you off their premises. Cold calling is tough. But if you can succeed here, the world is your oyster. And it is also possible to get lucky.

'In the early 1990s I was Commercial Manager at Huddersfield Town. Manager Eoin Hand asked me if I would try to get a sponsored car for new star signing 'Phil Starbuck'. At the time, Huddersfield Town did not have a friendly garage or a garage owner who was a keen Town fan (the best route) so I started from scratch.

Following my belief that any form of sponsorship must be truly beneficial to the Sponsor, I devised what I thought was a value-for-money package (see the proposal that follows). I met with Phil Starbuck, chatted through the sponsorship proposal and worked with him on how he should handle the sales presentation right from the first telephone call to the close of the sale.

My secretary produced the documentation, mail-merged letters and draft contracts, and within three weeks the meticulous planning and professional presentations got results. It was a thrill to see Phil drive onto the car park in a shining new Volvo ... only to be followed by Graham Mitchell (another

Town player) in a brand new Alfa Romeo car with his sponsorship details splattered in luminous 2-foot high letters all over the sides.

Although Graham Mitchell had been at Town for about eight years at that time, neither he nor any other player had managed to get a sponsored car. Graham was also one of the quieter ones in the squad, certainly not the type you would imagine could land an Alfa Romeo. How had he managed it?

A couple of weeks later I was at a luncheon in Huddersfield, and across the room I saw the owner of the Alfa Romeo dealership. I just had to ask him. After some small talk, I asked him outright, "By the way, David, how did Graham Mitchell persuade you to give him a sponsored car?"

His reply was amazing. "It was funny really," he said, "he just walked in and said, 'I don't suppose you would let me have a sponsored car, I play for Huddersfield Town. 'And I said to him, 'Yes, of course I can, I was wondering how long it would be before one of you lads walked in and asked me for a car.' It's good for my business to see one of my cars being driven around by a Huddersfield Town player."

It was as simple as that!'

As Woody Allen once said, 'Eighty-five per cent of success is turning up!'

The motto of the story is simple. Sponsorship can be found in the most unlikely of circumstances, but the golden rule is: if you don't ask, you don't get. I do not know how many garages Graham Mitchell had visited before he walked into the Alfa Romeo one and asked, 'Can I have a sponsored car?' but the result was just as effective as my professionally planned strategy.

5   Advertising
Places to advertise include:

a) Back Of Menu
This is explained in detail in Section 10, 'The Menu'. Without doubt, the menu is an excellent place to advertise for a sponsor.

b) On Your Dinner Letter
Offer a sponsorship package on the letter you send out selling tickets, or tables, to people on your hit-list.

c) In Your Match Programme

If yours is a sporting organisation, make sure an advertisement goes in the match programme outlining a sponsorship package.

d) Local Newspaper

Do not be scared to advertise in your local rag for a Sponsor. Make it an interesting package of benefits and you may get a buyer.

SPONSORSHIP CAR PROPOSAL

Phil Starbuck Proposal

New Car, Sales Promotion: Target, 12 new car sales per year

Phil Starbuck to provide:

1   Livery on vehicle: player name and company information.

2   Test drive for potential customers 2 afternoons per week if and when required.

3   Two complimentary tickets per match (home and away) for company's use (customers only) when required.

4   T-shirts with a company logo (for all individual press photographs).

5   Half-page advertisement during the season (photograph with owner of the first car sold).

6   Motor Group to have use of car for test driving when the player is out training (mornings).

7   Car to be driven around the pitch from 2.30-2.45 before 2 games per season.

8   Insurance of vehicle.

9   Free use of the club's facilities (if available) on 2 occasions per season, for seminars/sales meetings.

Motor Group to provide:

1   Free use of vehicle for 12 month period.

2   Road tax and servicing.

Part Four

THE BIG NIGHT

'Break a leg!'

17
The Room

Most functions have tables laid out in either 'sprigs' (or legs) or individual circular or square tables. It is always an advantage to have a long top table rather than expect your Speakers and Comedians to work from an ordinary circular or square table. To create a good atmosphere, arrange the individual tables or sprigs as near to the top table as possible.

At hotel venues, banqueting managers tend to spread the tables out around the room. This makes 'his' room look fuller and neater but it does not help 'your' night. Do not be afraid to tell him to rearrange the tables to your satisfaction.

Another thing they do is to leave the dance-floor area (just in front of the top table) empty, and arrange all the tables around the outskirts of the room. This is common at mixed functions when there is dancing after the formalities. While this may suit the banqueting manager, it is hard on your entertainers. Once again, do not be afraid to tell him to rearrange the room to your satisfaction. If necessary, he can move tables back from the dance floor later. It will ruin his night – but make yours. Do not settle for his laziness.

IOT
Tell the Banqueting Manager to set the room how you want it. You are paying the bill.

Table Plans

Unless the function is very informal, and you do not have any Sponsors to worry about, it is always a good idea to have a table plan. The best time to finalise it is about five hours before the function, say at lunchtime before an evening dinner. But be prepared for some cancellations right up until the moment the function begins. There are three basic options to consider.

1   A large A1-sized white card which shows each table numbered (or lettered) and indicates where each guest is to sit. This plan could be displayed near the entrance of the room, preferably on an easel.

2   This card not only displays how the tables are laid out but also has an alphabetical guest list informing each guest of his table number (eg Murphy J – Table 19).

3   This shows either the table plan and/or the alphabetical list but is photocopied on A4 sheets and distributed around the reception rooms prior to the function.

Option 3 is always good for large functions of 200+. If only one large table plan is displayed, as in Option 1, this can create a bottleneck as every guest waits in turn to view the plan. This can incur long delays.

When you finalise your table plan, be prepared to make some enemies. You can make most of your guests happy most of the time ... but whoever you seat furthest from the top table knows he is the least important person in the room! One way round this is to inform everyone (when you write announcing the function) that tables will be allocated when bookings are confirmed – so, to get a good table, book early. Do not think for one minute that you should operate such a system, but it gives you a good excuse when your unhappy guests complain that they could not hear or see the entertainment.

Locating the Top Table

Most rooms have a fixed layout arranged around a stage or performing area. There is only one golden rule: never put a top table in front of a bar.

Your top table should always be directly opposite the bar or entrance door. The reason for this is quite simple. If your guests are seated facing a top table which has only a wall behind it, they are not distracted by other activities going on in front of them. Whereas, if your guests are also facing a bar or windows, entrance doors, toilets, etc, they are easily distracted by people walking around.

> 'I was once a dinner guest at a Premier League Club (which will remain anonymous) where the top table had a walkway behind it. This was not too bad while the meal was being served, but once the Speakers were on their feet it was very distracting to see the waitresses continually walking behind the Speaker towards the bar. One particular waitress, about nineteen, with wobbly bits like Pamela Anderson, caused extra-special interest. It was great for the audience, but bad for the Speakers.'

In a long, narrow room it is usually best to put your top table in the centre against one of the long walls. It is important to seat the majority of your guests near the top table, and if it is in the centre of a narrow room this puts 60 per cent of guests near it as against 40 per cent if the top table is located at one end of the room.

Do You Need a Stage?

The size of the audience can determine whether you need some kind of stage. For an attendance around the 100-150 mark a raised stage is not necessary, but if you are expecting 500-600 guests a raised top table is a good idea. The perfect stage is about 18in high. This height just about keeps the top table and entertainers in view of the room, without losing intimacy. If a stage is too high, you lose this intimacy to a point where your entertainers look to be preaching down at the audience.

Do not be tempted to locate your top table on a theatre-type stage, even if it is built into the room. These stages are for concerts, pantomimes and the local dramatic society. You will have a much more friendly atmosphere if your entertainers are located in the body of the audience.

IOT
If you feel a built-in stage is too high, do not be scared to locate your top table at floor level in front of it. This will create more intimacy and atmosphere.

Spotlights

Some Sportsman's Dinners are held in function rooms designed predominantly for cabaret entertainment, and where it is usual to have a bank of spotlights to illuminate the stage when the room is darkened. This is not something you want at sporting dinners.

Although it can improve the atmosphere to dim the lights a little when the speeches begin, it is advisable not to use spotlights to illuminate the top table. Many Speakers look for eye contact with the audience, and this would be lost under spotlights. They can also make Speakers freeze like the proverbial rabbit in the car headlights.

IOT
Before a dinner at a new venue, always check out the top-table lighting.

Microphone Stands

Lecterns raised on a special podium are not generally used at Sportsman's Dinners, where your Celebrity is better positioned to address the audience from his place at the top table. However, a table-top lectern, on which your Speaker places his notes, can certainly be helpful.

As for microphones and microphone stands, there are three standard types. You can have a microphone mounted on a floor stand (either vertical or angled) which is positioned in front of the top table; or you can have it on a table stand, which allows your Speaker to operate hands-free, or you can choose a microphone which fits into a holder. Personally, I find the last type neither use nor ornament. Ask your venue to provide a suitable microphone and stand. If you are unfamiliar with them, make sure someone is available to instal and test it for you, and explain to you how it works, before any guests arrive.

Table Decorations

A well-decorated table is always a sound investment. When booking your function at a hotel, or planning your own event at the clubhouse, consider 'the look' of the room.

Flowers always look wonderful in the centre of the table, but if they prove too expensive a good effect can be created by matching tablecloths and napkins. If you have flowers, make sure that they are not in tall vases, otherwise your guests will find them troublesome as they try to chat across the table.

You can feature the club colours if they are suitable (not too much of the Harlequins effect!). Use them in conjunction with balloons filled with helium to make an interesting table decoration. Arrange six or seven balloons, in club colours, in a cluster and raised about 3ft from the centre of the table, just high enough for the guests to talk below them, or have one balloon tied to the back of each chair. There are two things to remember: firstly, try to get the balloons sponsored, and secondly do not use balloons if your room has a very high ceiling. You can bet on one of your guests cutting the string for a laugh and seeing the balloons rise to the ceiling, after which a clown from every other table will follow suit.

Table Gifts

Free gifts are always well received. Even though the gift is a 25p DD Golf Club biro, you will not find any around at the end of the night. No, not everyone will take them, but the local magpie (often a judge, politician or estate agent) will wait for his moment to collect all the remaining free gifts ... and menus ... and salt and pepper pots and any bits of cutlery still lying around!

A gift does not have to be expensive, it can be a pen, pencil, rubber, memo pad, fixture list, credit-card holder, etc. Make sure your gift carries some advertising, either for the club or the Sponsor. Ask your Sponsor if he would like to provide table gifts.

For his own guests, the Sponsor may like to provide a gift from his company. This obviously needs to be more substantial; ideas include cuff-links, special tie, diary, golf balls, minature bottle of brandy, Parker pen. Alternatively, the gift could be something for the guest to take home to his wife, eg perfume, brooch, gift voucher, chocolates, miniature liqueur, etc. The more expensive the gift, the better it works as a 'peace-offering' when your guest arrives home well sloshed at 2am.

£MT
If your club is a professional sports organisation, ask your
Sponsor for a budget per guest so you can purchase gifts
for them from your club shop.

Tapes, Books and Photographs

Some Speakers bring along with them audiotapes, books or photographs to sell to your audience at the end of the night. They may even take the opportunity to advertise their product as part of their speech. Out of courtesy, the Speaker/Comedian should ask the organisers' permission before selling their wares. If you feel strongly that the evening is designed to raise funds for your club, not the Speaker, do not be afraid to say no.

Alternatively, you can ask for 'corkage' and get a percentage of every sale for your club.

Other Points to Remember

1   Cloakroom
It is always a good idea to allocate a place for hanging coats, leaving umbrellas, etc, especially if your function is held between the months of October and March. At a hotel venue this is not usually a problem, but if necessary consider hiring portable hanging rails for this purpose.

2   Parking
If your venue is located in an area with a 'car theft' problem, consider employing a couple of students to welcome and park your guests arriving by car. Provide them with fluorescent yellow jackets. They can then 'police' the car parking until the evening is over. It will deplete the evening's profits by a few pounds, but such attention to detail will pay dividends if your function is an annual event.

3   Taxis
Consider whether any of your guests will require a taxi to get them home at the end of the night. If there are no public phones and the hotel reception has closed for the night, you could have a few frustrated guests. To avoid this, make sure that one of your committee brings along a portable phone so you can easily ring the local taxi company.

18
The Running Order

Another key element, often forgotten in the hubbub of organising everything, is a simple running order (see also Section 1, 'The Checklist'). On a number of occasions I have attended functions where the organiser has admitted, 'We forgot to do the raffle ... ha ha ha!' At the end of a successful evening this may not seem too important, but the financial implications of forgetting an important fund-raiser are enormous. It is also essential for the caterers, Speakers/Comedians and raffle-ticket sellers to know precisely when they are expected to begin.

In addition, you should schedule some natural breaks to allow guests to visit the toilet. A good general rule is: one break every 45 minutes after the meal.

The reason for this is quite simple. During the meal guests can leave to use the toilet when they wish. Once the Speaker begins, however, many are embarrassed to leave their seats, or do not want to distract the Speaker or Comedian. They can also become a prime target for the Comedian as they walk to the toilet: '... can see he doesn't spend a lot on clothes' ... 'not often you see flares nowadays'.

Beer drinkers may have four, five or six pints inside them, and after a boring Speaker who has rambled on for 55 minutes, their bladders are bursting. Only an inexperienced Compere continues the evening without proper breaks.

On the next page you will find a detailed running order. Photocopy the sheet and write in your own intended schedule.

Running Order (Dinner advertised as 7.00 for 7.30pm)

Time	Actual		Person's Name
6.00			
6.15			
6.30		Sponsors/Celebrity Guests Reception	
6.45			
7.00			
7.15		Call for people to be seated	Compere
7.30		Everyone seated – Grace	Local vicar
7.45		Serve meal	
8.00		Sell draw tickets (during soup course)	
8.15		Introduce Top Table	Compere
8.30			
8.45			
9:00		Loyal Toast	Team captain
9.15		Sell raffle tickets (during sweet course)	4 raffle sellers
9.30			
9.45		First Speaker	Dougie Doings
10.00			
10.15		Break for 10 minutes	
10.25		Draw prize	Guest of Honour
10.30		Second Speaker	Dougie Doings
10.45			
11.00		Break for 10 minutes	
11.15		Draw raffle (11.10)	Team manager
11.30		Comedian	Dougie Doings
11.45			
12.00		Auction	Compere
12.15		End of function – Thank-you	Chairman
12.30			
12.45			
1am			

This example shows an average function with two Speakers, three fund-raisers and a Comedian. Fill in the 'actual' time column as the night proceeds. If the evening runs overtime, you can see what caused the delay and correct it next time.

If all that is too detailed for you, here is a more straightforward running order, used at a dinner at Blackburn Rovers FC in 1997.

EVENING ITINERARY

1	WELCOME THE TOP TABLE
2	GRACE – MR GORDON TAYLOR (PFA)
3	FIRST COURSE MEAL
4	HOSTESSES COLLECT MONIES (£10) FOR RAYMON WEIL WATCH
5	DRAW FOR WATCH BY COLIN HENDRY & PRESENTATION
6	MAIN COURSE MEAL
7	HOSTESSES COLLECT MONIES FOR PREMIER SELECT XI
8	SWEET COURSE OF MEAL
9	LOYAL TOAST – MR HOWARD KENDALL
10	ANNOUNCEMENT OF WINNER OF PREMIER LEAGUE SELECT XI & PRESENATION – MR BILLY BINGHAM
11	CHEESE AND BISCUITS, COFFEE & MINTS
12	HOSTESSES COLLECT MONIES FOR RAFFLE
13	MEMORIAL ADDRESS FROM JOHN O'CONNOR & GERRY FARRELL
14	SPEAKER: MR PAUL FLETCHER
15	PRESENTATION OF RAFFLE – JIM SMITH, ETC.
16	COMEDIAN: MR MIKE KING
17	AUCTION OF SHIRTS & PRINTS
18	THANKS FROM V O'KEEFE

The Running Order in Detail

6.30   Reception (for Sponsors, Top Table, Celebrity Guests or Guest of Honour) Irrespective of whether or not your function is sponsored (and a private Sponsors Reception is held beforehand), it is always advisable to arrange for a small private room where your top table guests can gather before the event. This gives your important guests the chance to mix with the special Celebrity Guests in a quiet, controlled atmosphere, and also helps the organisers to check that all the top table guests have arrived. See that a guest list is made available, and have a committee member or commissionaire on the door.

7.15   Start to Get your Guests Seated

If you advertise your function as 7.00 for 7.30pm, start to get the early arrivals to their tables at 7.20 to start promptly at 7.30. Even though only 90 per cent of guests will have arrived at this time, it is essential to start on time. If it is your first dinner, start as you mean to continue, on time and on schedule. Ninety-five per cent of your guests will thank you for this. The longer you wait for people, the later they will be next time. Habitual late-comers will always arrive late, irrespective of advertised timings.

IOT

Do not be influenced by late-comers.

'I once attended a function where the event, advertised at 7.00 for 7.30pm, started at 9.15pm because Dougie Doings, the first-team captain, did not arrive on time! The end result was not that the meal was spoiled for the other 249 guests; or that the Speakers rushed and did not perform as well as usual; or that the organisers missed out one of the fund-raisers; or that the Comedian was angry because he was booked for Thursday night and he got introduced on Friday morning. The important thing in this situation is that some guests will get home too late and WILL NOT COME AGAIN.

And all because we had to wait for Dougie, who's a 'great bloke' and a 'real character', and was still there at 3.30 in the morning, stoned out of his head .... In his case this was probably because, unlike everyone else in the room, he did not have to work the next day.'

IOT

Start on time.

God Save The Queen

Bedale Football Club's dinner in North Yorkshire is the only function where I have heard the National Anthem played to start the proceedings. Even though the tune was played on an old crackling 78 record, it was received with great respect and I even saw a few salutes from the older generation.

7.30   Grace and Welcome

It is courteous to start the dinner formally with Grace. It can be said by the Compere, or a nice touch is for a local vicar, celebrity, dignitary, politician (always looking for acknowledgment) or the Club Chairman to say Grace. The usual formula is as follows:

Compere: 'Gentlemen please be upstanding whilst we say Grace ....'
Chosen Speaker: 'For what we are about to receive, may the Lord make us truly thankful. AMEN.'

(see page 187 at the end of this section for a selection of Graces I have heard in many different parts of the country.)

7.45   Serve the Meal

Background music is always a nice touch. Now is the time for the musicians to move around the tables.

8.15   Introduce the Top Table

It should be regarded as an honour to sit on the top table. The main people who should be invited on to the top table are:

The main Speaker/s – *obviously.*
The Comedian – *if he is arriving for dinner.*
The Club Chairman – *unless he wishes to sit with his guests.*
The Compere – *of course.*
The Team Manager – *if it is a team function.*
The Guest of Honour – *who may not be speaking.*
Local Politician – *usually only if he is an MP or Council Leader, otherwise it may seem that the evening has political undertones.*
Club dignitary/Secretary/Captain elect/President/ Sponsor, etc.

People to avoid having on the top table:

Friends/relatives of anybody – *this relationship does not earn them the right to sit on the top table.*
The Groundsman – *unless he is to be acknowledged for a special reason.*
The Organiser – *should sit close to the Compere on a separate table.*
Anyone not wearing a tie – *if the evening requires a tie to be worn.*
Anyone with a reputation for bad behaviour, barracking, drunkenness, etc.

The top table is everyone's focus for the evening and should have an element of mystique. Guests should 'earn the right' to sit on the top table. A sloppy top table projects an image of sloppy organisation. At many functions, the top table will be held back in their Reception room and officially 'clapped-in', with the Compere announcing their arrival as follows:

Compere: 'Gentlemen, please be upstanding to welcome your top table guests.'

If you decide to do this at your function, here are some simple guidelines:

* Have place cards in position, otherwise the top table will look disorganised in front of the whole room as they all wonder where to sit, and your Star Celebrity may finish up sitting at the end of the table.
* Line up your top table in sitting order outside the room.
* Decide which route the leader should take, otherwise he may wander around the room and get on stage from the wrong side.
* Instruct the leader either to get on the stage from the right and walk to sit at the far left, or vice versa.
* Remember to hold back a special Guest of Honour.

Keep the Mystique
Nobody should 'work' on the top table. The top table is not the place to do any administrative tasks, especially counting money or tearing up raffle tickets. In fact, it is extremely rude for anyone sitting on the top table to be

reading, writing or counting money, above all when the Speakers and Comedian are on their feet.

Whenever possible, the top table should play their part in the evening's entertainment. As the top table is the focal point of the room, it adds greatly to the atmosphere if top table guests are seen to be laughing, listening intently to the speeches and enjoying themselves.

Introducing Your Special Guests

If the top table is genuinely reserved for your VIP Guests, it is always a good idea to introduce them to the audience. This can be an informal introduction either in between courses, during the meal or just before your first Speaker. It can also be a good opportunity to introduce:

*   A new Manager or Coach
*   A new Sponsor
*   The Team Captain
*   Local VIP (businessman, politician or vicar, etc)
*   The Club Chairman

These introductions should be short and sweet (although it could be a good opportunity for a talented Compere to have a go at some of the VIP Guests):

'Please welcome Club Chairman and local alcoholic ... MR DOUGIE DOINGS ... What a lovely blazer, Mr Chairman. When I first arrived I thought you were a coach driver!'

'I once attended a function at a golf club in Hampshire where the Club President was asked to introduce the top table prior to the speeches. He had obviously done his homework because he had a two-page biography on each of his guests. As there were 16 people on the top table these introductions took nearly two hours. This is no exaggeration. The function ended at 1.45am.'

IOT
Top table introductions should be short and sweet.

Speakers' Introduction

This is NOT the time to give a detailed introduction of your Guest Speakers. That can come as part of the build-up before they speak. Just a simple acknowledgment is sufficient. All a competent Compere needs to say is something like this:

'On my immediate left, please welcome our main Celebrity Guest this evening, who I will introduce formally a little later ... MR DOUGIE DOINGS.'

The Guest of Honour

Only a handful of people in each sport or occupation can be truly classed as a Guest of Honour. While a member of the Royal Family would automatically be acknowledged in this way, it is important that any sporting figure so honoured should indeed be special.

For example, in East Lancashire footballing circles, Sir Tom Finney and Nat Lofthouse, OBE often adorn the top table; they are not only living legends but, more importantly, perfect gentlemen. At many functions, and not only in the Stoke area, Sir Stanley Matthews is in regular attendance as a true Guest of Honour. I have often had the pleasure of his company, and, as a Bolton lad and ex-Bolton player, I am familiar with the folklore surrounding Sir Stan and the infamous Bolton Wanderers defender, Tommy Banks.

'In my Commercial Manager days in the late 1980s I helped to organise a function at the Dunkenhalgh Hotel in Accrington in 1989, when Sir Stanley was Guest of Honour at Colne Dynamos FC annual dinner. A packed room of over 350 dinner-suited guests had just 'clapped in' the top table, and Sir Stan had been kept back for a special welcome. As everyone sat down and started to chat, Compere Mike King, with the timing of a true pro, quietly announced: "Gentlemen, I am proud to welcome Sir Stanley Matthews, MBE."

A quietness fell over the audience while this incredibly fit, white-haired legend nimbly walked into the room. His twinkle-toe patent-leather shoes could be heard on the ballroom floor when he first entered, and, as he walked past the first table, unprompted, the whole table stood up and started to applaud. As did the next table, and on it went like a wave across the room. By the time Sir Stan had shuffled and side-stepped his way to the middle of the room, all 350 people were on their feet, and by the time this genius of 80 years old had reached the top table, the roar of the cheering was deafening.

This unplanned, spontaneous welcome ovation lasted four minutes and was truly a wonderful moment for everyone who had the good fortune to be there on that very special night. I do not mind admitting a few tears rolled down my cheeks as the audience paid tribute to one of football's legends.

At the end of the night, Sir Stan asked if he and his driver, Jackie Moody, could sell a few coffee mugs to anyone who "may" want Stan's autograph. The mugs had Sir Stan's career history embossed on the side. Once the function had ended, the two of them opened for business, and for the next hour I have never seen money change hands so quickly. I did not count how many empty boxes, each containing 24 mugs, were left on stage at the end of the evening. And I will not try to guess how many mugs were sold that night at £10 each, but the constant queue was never shorter than a penalty kick. I only hope the crafty old silver fox made lots and lots of money. He brought so much pleasure to so many people at a time when footballers were not well paid. He deserves every penny he can make now!

At a function in Alsager in late 1997, when Stan was 83 years old, he really surprised me when I asked him about his playing days. At first I thought he was pulling my leg, but as we talked I discovered he was deadly serious. We started with small talk about Bolton Wanderers and his beloved Stoke City, and then I asked him, "Looking back, Stan, have you any regrets?"

Without a second thought he said, "Oh yes, I retired too early." I really believed he was joking, well aware that he was 53 when he retired. I also remembered reading that he won his second 2nd Division Championship medal 30 years after winning his first.

Then he said something that made me realise I was probably sitting next to one of the most outstanding athletes of this century. He said, "Do you know, Paul, in my day we didn't have the benefit of the medical knowledge that today's players do. I had my first cartilage out after being injured in an Over-35s match when I was 71. The keyhole surgery was superb and I was in and out of hospital in no time. It took me a while to get over it, and although I got back playing a couple of years later (73) do you know ... I was never quite the same after that." He just shrugged his shoulders and carried on eating.'

9.00   The Loyal Toast

The Loyal Toast traditionally announces to guests that they are now formally allowed to smoke after their meal. A simple method of introducing it is as follows:

Compere: 'Gentlemen, would you please be upstanding and charge your glasses while I call upon your Chairman, Mr Dougie Doings, to propose the Loyal Toast.'
(Everyone stands.)
Chairman: 'Gentlemen, The Queen.'
All guests: 'The Queen.'
Compere: 'Gentlemen, you now have your Chairman's permission to smoke.'

There are of course many variants of the Toast. In Lancashire they often say, 'The Queen, Duke of Lancashire.' This could cause offence outside Lancashire, and is not recommended beyond the county of the red rose.

Things can go wrong too. In Norwich I once heard an extremely nervous Chairman, panic-stricken at having to propose a toast in front of 500 guests, have a total block and announce the Loyal Toast as follows: 'For what we are about to receive, the Queen ... and a Duke.' Believe it or not, this received a standing ovation from a packed audience, all familiar with the fear of public speaking.

Smoking

Nowadays smoking is not as acceptable as it used to be. Since the discovery of 'passive smoking' and secondary smoke-related illnesses, the days of the smoke-filled room with yellow ceilings are probably gone forever. Often people will now ask permission to smoke before lighting a cigarette or cigar, and this change of attitude is prevalent at large functions. Usually it is covered by the Compere. A few examples are:

'You now have your Chairman's permission to smoke ... on the car park!'
'You now have your Chairman's permission to ask the person sat next to you if you have his permission to smoke!'

'You now have the Chairman's permission to continue smoking!'
'You now have the Government's permission to smoke, once you have read their warning on the packet.'
'You can now smoke, or go up in ******* flames if you want to!'

'One famous smoker on the circuit is a very talented Comedian called Mike Farrell from Keighley, West Yorkshire. He has been known to go through a pack of twenty during his act, and often uses a puff of a cigarette to accentuate a joke. I once drove Mike to Oxford to speak at Oxford United Football Club, and it was like driving through four hours of fog in mid-August.

On another occasion ex-international cricketer Mike Cowan, a superb Speaker, and I found Mike Farrell in a state of despair and verging on suicide at 7.45pm, just before a function at the Ponderosa Hotel in Doncaster.

"Whatever's the matter?"

"I've given up smoking," was Mike's shaky reply.

"When did you stop?" we asked.

"Half past three ... this afternoon!"

By 9.15pm he was back on the weed.'

9.30 Speakers and Fund-raisers

If you want to finish before midnight, and you have two Speakers and a Comedian, it is important to have your first Speaker on his feet before 10pm, preferably a little earlier. If your function has only one Speaker and a Comedian, or two Speakers, 10pm is a good time to start the entertainment.

IOT
If you have not heard him before, ask your Speaker how long he usually speaks for. If he says 90 minutes, insist that he works to your timings. A speech of 35-45 minutes is perfectly adequate.

You can go straight into introducing your first Speaker immediately after the top table introductions, although the more usual time is after the Loyal Toast. Whichever you choose, there is one golden rule to check on: make sure all the waiters/waitresses have finished clearing the table. There are two reasons for this. Firstly, your caterers will normally like to clear all the cups, plates and saucers from the tables so all the waiters/waitresses can be paid and go home. If this cannot be done before the Speaker begins, they all have to wait for over 30 minutes and sit through the speech. Secondly, if you allow the tables to be cleared while your Speaker is on his feet, this can easily cause distractions. It is also bad manners and the Speaker will not thank you for it.

IOT
Make sure all the tables are cleared of plates, coffee cups, etc, before you introduce your first Speaker.

Bars and Waiter Service
To help the night go well, postpone bar service during the speeches, again out of courtesy to your Speakers. For those who want to order drinks, it is easy to raise a hand and silently summon a waiter, or a pad and pen can be left on the table and used to write down drinks orders.

Then you just have to ask the Compere to announce: 'The bars will be closed during the speeches, but if you want to order drinks, you will find a pad and pen on your table. Write down your order and give it to the waiter. Thank you.'

Breaks
It is important to have a break somewhere between 10pm and the end of the evening. A good Compere will know exactly when, and how long, to have a break in proceedings to allow the guests to visit the toilets.

He will also know at what point to bring in your fund-raisers. It is obviously important not to draw the raffle, or play Stand-up Bingo, during the break periods as up to 40 per cent of the guests are away from their tables. A good running order after 9.30pm is:

Coffee
Break (10-15 minutes)
Game
First Speaker
Break (5 minutes)
Raffle draw
Comedian (or second Speaker)
Auction.

12.00   The Chairman's Thanks

At the end of the evening it is always a good idea for someone briefly to say thank-you to the guests for attending. This can be very risky if left in the wrong hands. If you are organising the event, do not ask the chairman to wind up the evening without giving strict instructions.

Many an excellent evening has been ruined by a drunken chairman, president or manager trying to steal the limelight by telling jokes or rambling on. Obviously, if the chairman is a real wit and well used to delivering such a speech, it can only add to a great night. But if not, make sure the thank-you is brief.

For example:

'Gentlemen, I hope you will agree this has been a wonderful evening and it is an extremely important one for DD Football Club. Your support is vital to our club's success and I thank you most sincerely for attending this evening.

   To our Speakers (Dougie Doings and Dougie Doings), Comedian (Dougie Doings) and Compere (Dougie Doings) I pass on my thanks and also to our Sponsors and Guests who have taken part in our fund-raisers.

   I look forward to seeing you all again next year and hope you will keep a watchful eye on our progress up until then. Thank you.'

A speech like that is short, sweet and allows guests to get on to one of three important places: the bar, the toilet, or their wife (who is outside waiting in the car).

Sixty Glorious Graces

1   I hope this food is what you like,
    'Cos its been blessed by David Icke.

2   Bread is a lovely thing to eat
    God bless the barley and the wheat
    A lovely thing to breathe is air
    God bless the sunshine everywhere
    The earth's a lovely place to know
    God bless the folks that come and go!
    Alive's a lovely thing to be
    Giver of life – we say – bless thee!

3   He who eats and drink his fill
    Then belches with relief
    But does not bless the Lord with thanks
    Is best described a thief.

4   O Gentle Jesus, friend of mine,
    Who turneth water into wine
    Please forgive these foolish men,
    Here to turn it back again.

5   Lord of mercy
    Bless our food
    Keep us in a pleasant mood.

    Bless the chef
    And those who serve us
    From indigestion
    Lord preserve us.

So with sighs
And bursting breeches
We may fall asleep
During the boring speeches.

Lord this plea comes from
Saint and Sinners
And all 'local character' mates
On subsidised dinners.

6   Lord bless this hungry gathering
     May your food fill them up
     We've ordered meals for eighty-seven
     And ninety-five's turned up.

7   We love a competition
     Do me and Eric and Bob,
     And once we've had this meal tonight
     We'll guess the chef's real job.

8   For what we are about to receive
     And for what some have already snatched
     Especially those who have eaten their breadroll
     May the Lord make us truly thankful.

9   It is with thanks and happiness
     We eat here with elation
     But more importantly than food, O Lord
     Save us from relegation.

10   The Lord be praised
     My belly's raised
     An inch above the table
     And I'll be damned
     If I'm not crammed
     As full as Auntie Mabel.

11   Look down upon us who are gathered here
     As we thank you for good food and beer
     Old Hall parents, guests and staff
     We have come to feast and drink and laugh.

12   A new tennis court is our desire
     The cost of which rises ever higher
     Two and twenty pounds we've paid
     To ensure that the game is played
     On a surface that is smooth and true
     Where a bump or a crack would never do
     A perfect venue for ball and racquet ...
     Unfortunately it will cost a packet!

13   Look kind on our guests tonight
     May their words be clever, wise, not trite.
     A former Burnley and England star
     A frequent visitor to the bar
     To Telford we welcome Mr Paul Fletcher
     If he drinks too much he will leave on a stretcher
     He entertained thousands at Turf Moor
     And us I'm sure he will not bore
     Mr Sid Tate our courtly jester
     Praised as far a-field as Leicester
     His stories, quips and jests and jokes
     Should appeal to all, especially blokes.

14   And so good Lord please bless us all
     The fat, the thin, the large, the small
     In fellowship we share this meal
     In gratitude to you we kneel.

15   Gracious, O Lord, are thy gifts of food and drink
     Gracious, too, this place where we enjoy them.
     Let gratitude fill our hearts with joy
     Through Jesus Christ our Lord. Amen.

16   Thank you, Lord, as we sit here
      With feast and fire and nought to fear
      Pity the unhappy poor
      And bless this house for evermore
      Through Jesus Christ, Amen.

17   Thanks for breakfast, lunch and dinner
      If it weren't for you, I'd be much thinner.

18   **A Scottish Grace**
      Never spend 10 words
      When three will do
      Eat, drink, Amen.

19   **'After Thanks'**
      For what we have received
      we are truly thankful. Amen.

20   **The Chairman's Grace**
      Our Chairman is a kindly chap
      He's jolly fun and bright
      He hopes that you will enjoy yourselves
      Although the food is shite.

      He's generous and wealthy too
      And so full of good cheer
      But when the raffle comes around
      Just watch him disappear.

      And once the night is over
      And all the speeches said
      You'll find him in the corner
      Pissed out of his head.

      If you see him in the car park
      Spewing up his guts

Please pick him up and dust him down
And kick him in the nuts.

21   God bless this bunch
As we munch our lunch
I have a hunch
The night has punch.

22   We thank thee, Father, for thy care
Food, friends, and kindliness we share
May we forever mindful be
Of Club and Country and of thee.

23   For every cup and plateful
God make us truly grateful. Amen.

24   **If**
If the company is as pleasant as the food
And the food is as tasty as the Speakers
And the Speakers are as warm as the wine
And the wine is as fruity as the waitresses
And the waitresses are as randy as the Chairman
We're in for a good night – Amen.

25   Bless the tiny piece of ham
Bless the lonely dab of jam
Bless the sparsely-buttered toast,
Father, Son and Holy Ghost.

26   **A Common Grace**
We thank Thee, Lord, for vulgar food,
For trotters, tripe, pig's cheek,
For steak and onions with their crude
But appetising reek.

Potatoes in their jackets make
Us plain folk honour Thee;
And Thou with us when we bake
Fresh shrimps for Sunday tea.

27 Give me a good digestion, Lord
And also something to digest
But when and how that something comes
I leave to thee, who knowest best.

28 Thy people's praise is overdue,
But see, dear Lord, we kneel
To offer thanks for Irish Stew
And tasty, cheap cowheel.

Now wait a minute, Lord! Don't miss
The last word on our lips:
We thank Thee most of all for this,
Thy gift of fish and chips.

29 Lord, bless this food upon these dishes
Like thou didst bless the loaves and fishes
And like the sugar in the tea
May all of us be stirred by thee.

30 As we assemble round the board
We do as did our Heavenly Lord
And for his Church our Lord Divine
Chose fellowship and bread and wine.

31 **Shortest Grace**
A teacher once asked his pupils to see who could write the shortest grace. The following Grace won the competition.

'Ta, Pa.'

32 For rabbits young and rabbits old,
    For rabbits hot and rabbits cold,
    For rabbits tender and rabbits tough,
    We thank thee, Lord: we've had enough.

33 O Lord, who blessed the loaves and fishes,
    Look doon upon these twa bit dishes,
    And though the tatties be but small,
    Lord, make 'em plenty for us all;
    But if our stomachs they do fill,
    'Twill be another miracle.

34 **The Selkirk Grace**
    Some hae meat and canna eat
    And some wad eat that want it.
    But we hae meat and we can eat,
    And sae the Lord be thankit.

35 For good food, good wine
    And good fellowship
    Lord we give our thanks.

36 God bless the Chairman of this club
    And bless his Missus too
    And all the Club's good Patrons
    Around the table, too
    Around the table, true good men
    And happy may they be
    Sing Father, Son and Holy Ghost
    For our Club's victory.

37 Thy Providence supplies my food,
    And 'tis Thy Blessing makes it good;
    My soul is nourished by Thy Word,
    Let soul and body praise the Lord.

38 Blessing to God, for ever blest,
    To God the Master of the feast,
    Who hath for us a table spread,
    And with his daily bounties fed;
    May he with all gifts impart
    The crown of all – a thankful heart.

39 **A Grace by Dr Alan Rebello**
    (A Blackburn Rovers Fan)
    Bless O Lord, this food we eat
    Bless all who at this table meet
    Enter each heart, that we may be
    In love and fellowship with thee. Amen.

40 We bless thee Lord for this our food,
    But more for Jesus' Flesh and Blood,
    The manna to our spirits given,
    The living Bread sent down from Heaven.

    Praise shall our grateful lips employ:
    While life and plenty we enjoy.
    Till worthy, we adore Thy Name,
    While banqueting with Christ the Lamb.

41 We bless thee, Lord, for this our food
    For life and health and every good
    May we more blest than we deserve
    Live less for self and more to serve.

42 God blease our meate,
    God guide our waies,
    God give us grace
    Our Lord to please.
    Lord longe p'serve in peace and health
    Our gracious Queene Elizabeth.

43 Almighty God, Eternal Kinge
W'ch madest Heaven and ev'ry thinge:
Graunte unto us that present be
To taste the foode that heire we see.

44 **A Cricket Grace**
For food and drink
And bat and ball
We thank the Lord
We love them all.

45 Then shall we find it true indeed
God will forsake us never,
But helpe us when we have most nede,
To Whom we praise for ever. Amen.

46 Now we have bouth meate and drinke,
Our bodies to sustayne;
Let us remember helpesse folke,
Who need doth cause to pine.
And like God is merciful
To us givynge such store;
So let us now be pittiful
In helping of the poor.

47 **For Jeremy**
Ashes to ashes
Dust to dust
If you'd have stuck to women
You'd still be here with us.

48 **A Football Grace**
He plays at weekends with the lads
Weather, windy, fine or raining
When he's not involved in League or Cup
He's off for extra training.

But it's not the game of football
That attracts him to the club
It's the way we work together
Getting plastered at the pub.

49   **A Rotary Grace**
O Lord and giver of all good
We thank thee for our daily food
May Rotary aims and Rotary ways
Help us to serve thee all our days.

50   **A Rugby Union Grace**
Lord let us remember
Those less fortunate than ourselves
The hungry who live below the poverty line
Those oppressed who live behind the enemy line
The Welsh who live behind their own try-line.

51   **Round Table**
May we O Lord
Adopt thy creed
Adapt our ways
To serve thy need.

And we who on
Thy bounty feed
Improve in thought
In word and deed.

52   **For an Association**
Bless our food
Bless our fellowship
And Lord bless the aims of our association.

53   Thank you for the world so sweet
Thank you for the food we eat

Thank you for the birds that sing
Thank you, God, for everything.

54   May the grace of Christ our Saviour
And the Father's boundless love
With the Holy Spirit's favour
Rest upon us from above.

55   Give us Lord a bit o' sun
A bit o' work and a bit o' fun
Give us all in struggle and sputter
Our daily bread (and a bit o' butter).

56   We thank thee, Lord, for happy hearts
For rain and sunny weather
We thank thee, Lord, for this our food
And that we are together.

57   Praise to God who giveth meat
Convenient unto all to eat
Praise for tea and buttered toast
Father, Son and Holy Ghost.

58   For what we're about to receive,
Has nowt to do wi' the ... Conservatives.
(or chairman, local villain, etc)

59   The pleasure of this meal tonight
As I sit beside this sinner
Our Chairman makes a lovely noise
As he sits and eats his dinner.

60   God is great and God is good
Let us thank him for this food
But don't forget our gracious Jean
Who cooks the food and screws the team.

Part Five

OTHER IDEAS

'Have you ever thought about .... ?'

19
The Toastmaster

What a wonderful sight to see a toastmaster, resplendent in a crisp white shirt, white bow tie and three-quarter-length 'hunting pink' jacket. His immaculate grey handlebar moustache is all part of the spectacle, as are his white waistcoat and gold watch and fob. This show of peacock finery provides colourful decoration behind the top table, and is an exhibition of opulence that can make your night ... or ruin it!

Although our toastmaster looks superb and can add to the prestige of a Royal Banquet or State Occasion, he may look a little out of place at Grimethorpe Rovers Under-14s annual football club dinner. A Sportsman's Dinner is not usually regarded as a formal occasion, and it is also very possible that a toastmaster will not be familiar with your sport or even your Celebrity Guest. Just imagine this introduction:

'Mr Chairman, Mr President, honoured guests and Gentlemen. It is now my privilege to introduce you to someone here to speak to you from the world of football. Your guest is Mr Norbert Styles, he once played in a football game which was called the World Cup Final at Wembley Stadium, and he was on the winning team ....'

If this type of introduction is done tongue in cheek, it may be acceptable, but such formal introductions are far better directed at a Member of Parliament or successful entrepreneur prior to a Chamber of Commerce trade luncheon than our friend Nobby, whose appearance now is that of a gentle florist, in contrast to the wild animal that roamed Old Trafford!

A toastmaster is also not really the right person to introduce a raffle, special draw or auction, which means these will have to be orchestrated at the microphone by someone else (and very rarely will a professional Compere be employed on the same bill as a toastmaster). It is not a good idea to leave your important fund-raisers in the hands of someone not familiar with how to capitalise on these events.

There appear to be between 300 and 500 professional or semi-professional toastmasters around. Many of them simply buy a red jacket, grow a handlebar moustache and advertise their services as 'toastmaster for all occasions'. These occasions could be weddings, company presentations, special events, etc. A toastmaster should be a member of a professional organisation such as the National Association of Toastmasters or belong to one of the many guilds and federations located around the country.

This will probably narrow your choice down to around 300 nationally, of whom probably less than 50 are experienced at Sportsman's Dinners. One toastmaster who is vastly experienced at such functions is John Cooke from Cheshire. He fully understands the philosophy of the whole event and throughout the evening is seen parading around the room, ensuring queries are answered and feeding back important information to the organiser. Once the speeches start, John stands quietly to one side of the top table, but his eagle eye is roaming the room while he enjoys a laugh at a funny story. With his impressive voice he makes numerous announcements throughout the evening, from 'Gentlemen, would you please take your seats for dinner' to '... can I wish you a safe journey home'.

IOT
Make sure your toastmaster is not only a member of a professional organisation but also has experience of Sportsman's Dinners ... or you could be booking a town crier by mistake.

To sum up, my recommendations are as follows:

*   Do not book a toastmaster for your first Sportsman's Dinner (unless you have invited the Queen). He may be too formal.

*   Think about having a Toastmaster if your dinner is well established, the tickets sell themselves, and you are looking for that 'something special' for the night.

*   Do not book a toastmaster and Compere on the same bill unless funds are there a-plenty and you are trying to create an impression.

*   Do not book a toastmaster unless you have seen him perform well at another function, or have had him recommended to you by someone you trust.

20
The Stripper

Probably the days of the stripper are gone forever. Praise the Lord! I hope we have also seen the back (sorry about the pun) of the Strippergram. Hallelujah! They are relics of the Sixties and Seventies, a time when the stand-up Comedian used to take a couple of girls along with him to titillate the audience after his 30-minute spot of blue jokes.

Somehow this seedy element crept into the Sporting Dinner scene, and you got 'Raquel from Scunthorpe' parading around the room rubbing body lotion into bald heads and flashing her cellulite legs and a body that was well past its sell-by date. Then followed the Strippergram when, as a real surprise, all your mates chipped in £5 to see a Policewoman with a whip read a pathetic poem before she stripped off and rubbed her boobs in your face.

A just-tolerable variant of the stripper is the strip auction. This is when a young lady stands at the front of the room, sometimes on top of the top table, and the auctioneer auctions off each item of her clothing. Because it can help raise club funds it is just about acceptable, but on the whole best avoided, unless of course you know a Pamela Anderson.

'In 1992 I was invited to be a guest Speaker for a football team in the Midlands. I drove down with the Comedian and the Compere, who will remain nameless. The function was in a room above a pub. There were about 80 men present, and it seemed a normal kind of night. The organiser asked whether we minded if, in-between the Speaker (me) and the Comedian, 'Sandra from Solihull' did a strip for the lads to help raise club funds. It seemed a bit seedy, but rather than spoil the fun we told them to get on with it. Once I was off-stage I went to have a coffee behind the bar, while Sandra pranced around taking off her clothes.

Fifteen minutes later, all three of us were back on-stage and the organiser asked if the Compere would announce that, if the lads put £5 in a pint glass, Sandra would perform another spot after the Comedian. What the hell, we thought, we would be on the M6 by the time she came back.

Forty-five minutes later, we were all in the manager's office saying our good-byes and we could hear the roar outside as Sandra did her second spot. As we walked through the room on our way out we saw a second bare bottom, quite obviously not Sandra's, up there on the stage. I will leave the rest to your imagination.

It was only the next morning that we realised the implications. A Sunday newspaper reporter was parked in the Compere's drive asking him to comment on last night's 'live sex show' in the Midlands. We all were obviously very worried, and fortunately managed to avoid the awful publicity that could have linked three seasoned professional Speakers to that sort of show. As a result, we have all vowed never to appear on the same bill as a stripper again.'

IOT
Do not book a stripper unless you have cleared it with your entertainers. They may refuse to work on the same bill.

21
The Alternative Theme

Most clubs and organisations aim to establish their Sportsman's Dinner on an annual, biannual or quarterly basis. They can then approach the same companies and individuals to buy tickets, confident that they and their guests will have an enjoyable evening.

Sometimes these organisations also have a one-off event using an alternative theme to the standard Sportsman's Dinner. These events can themselves become established as annual occasions, and in their own right provide a valuable form of fund-raising for the club.

There are a number of options, which have many elements in common with sporting dinners, such as raffles, auctions and prize draws, but the format for the evening is very different.

The Questions and Answers Night
(sometimes called a Sports Forum)

Some professional Speakers prefer not to stand and tell stories for 30 minutes and would rather answer questions from the floor. George Best and Rodney Marsh have been extremely successful at this type of event, regularly packing out function rooms throughout the country. Although their evenings usually work very well, the format is not without its hazards.

If the Speaker does not fancy standing up and talking in front of 200 people, why should the audience fancy standing up and asking questions in front of the same 200 people? The fear of public speaking also applies to people asking questions. That is, except for the village clown! Fired up with too many glasses of wine, he wants to bring attention to himself.

'Who's the best jump you've ever had, George, ha ha ha,' he asks, getting a cheap laugh out of the audience and insulting the Celebrity Guest.

For a Questions and Answers session to go well, you need three ingredients:

*   A competent Compere, who can shield the Celebrity Guest from the village idiot.
*   Some planted questions – just to get the ball rolling. These should be interesting questions that will encourage an interesting answer from your guest.
*   A roving microphone, radio mike or two microphones which will allow the questions to be heard as well as the answers.

If your celebrity guest has agreed to take part in a Questions and Answers session, do not be scared to ask him what questions he would like to be asked. If he has done it before, he should have a few stock answers and stories which he is happy to tell.

> 'One Speaker who often asks the audience if there are any questions after her speech is Cynthia Payne, Madam Sin, a very busy Speaker on the circuit. She has some wonderful anecdotes about her time running a London brothel, and I was quite surprised how entertaining her stories are, not the least bit offensive or smutty. I spoke at a luncheon with Cynthia in the Isle Of Man. The audience were mainly bankers, solicitors, estate agents, etc, all male, and Cynthia entertained them and answered their questions very well.
>
> Unfortunately, she gave me her business card and wrote on the back of it, "Thank you for your custom." It took quite a bit of explaining when my wife found it a few weeks later as she was sending my suits to the cleaners.'

Usually the Sports Forum does not include a formal meal, which obviously reduces costs. However, food can be made available on a bar-snacks basis. Tickets for a Sporting Questions Sports Forum or 'An Evening with Dougie Doings' can be sold at £5, £10, £15 or £20, depending on the cost of the Celebrity Guest. If the event is held at the club's own facilities, the bar takings will also contribute to the profit. Remember, the basic way to calculate profit is: sale of tickets + bar profits – cost of entertainment = profit.

The Boxing Dinner

I have only ever attended one Boxing Dinner as Guest Speaker, and that was in Derby in 1991. But I have heard many Comedians tell stories of how difficult it is to perform from the centre of a boxing ring, and trying to work to four sections of the audience.

Luckily, the Boxing Dinner I attended was a well-planned and well-established event, featuring young amateur boxers ranging in age from 11 up to 17 years old. The evening had a traditional top table and guests arrived in dinner jackets, but during the speeches the large boxing ring dominated the room and detracted from the atmosphere.

The Boxing Dinner appears to be complicated to arrange, costly, and not good for other performers, such as Speakers and Comedians. Its main appeal is clearly for audiences who enjoy watching a couple of fighters knock the hell out of each other.

The Race Night

Quite a few organisers around the country specialise in Race Nights. The horse races themselves can provide good entertainment for guests at a traditional dinner and are probably best as part of an evening's sporting dinner entertainment, rather than 'top of the bill'.

The horse races are prerecorded and projected on to a big screen. Usually they are races from America, Hong Kong or France, so that guests will not have any idea which horses won the races. The commentary is also recorded and begins when all bets have been taken. Winnings are distributed after the event, and a percentage of the takings pays for the cost of the entertainment.

Race Nights have been going on for many years but have never really established themselves as annual events for clubs and organisations. This probably means they never will. They make a good novelty night, something different, but, in horse language, do not have the staying power.

The Sportsman's Dinner without the Dinner

'In spring 1997 I spoke at a function in Driffield, East Yorkshire. It was a Sportsman's Dinner that had everything ... everything but the dinner.

The room was empty when I arrived at 7.25pm (the booking form said 7.30 for an 8.00 start). At 7.30 Seth Sheldon, a good Comedian from Sunderland, arrived. He told me he had worked the venue on many occasions over the last twenty years and promised a good night.

At 7.45 Tommy Docherty walked in. "Have we got the night wrong," he said, "where is everybody?" The organiser arrived at 7.50, bought the three of us a drink and told us about the night.

"We usually get about 300 men and all they like to do is have a good drink and hear a few football stories. There will be fans of Hull City (one of the many clubs Tommy Docherty managed), Leeds United, Middlesborough and the usual half-dozen Man United fans. Just go up on stage at about 8.30, tell a few good stories and you'll be away by 11.30. Last year we had Emlyn Hughes, Steve Kindon and Jimmy Bright and they were great. I can promise you a good evening."

If my calculations were correct, when I had deducted the expenditure from the income, the club's profits were around about £1750 plus the profit from the bar takings, which must have been over £2500 on the night.'

Sporting Club Groups

Karl Ward founded his Sporting Club group in 1991. It organises four quarterly Sportsman's Dinners in towns and cities around the Midlands. Unlike the traditional Sportsman's Dinner, all Sporting Club dinners follow a precise format. Companies and individuals join the club as members, and then are allowed to bring guests to the annual dinner.

The Dinners themselves focus on entertainment, not fund-raising, and all profits from a fund-raising event, such as a raffle, go directly to a nominated local charity. The evening has a Chairman, usually a well-known celebrity such as ex-cricketer Tom Graveney, and dress is strictly bow tie. On a typical evening, two celebrity sporting Speakers and a Master of Ceremonies, such as David Duckham MBE (who is superb at the job), provide the evening's entertainment. To add that little bit of class, a resplendent red-coated toastmaster is always on hand from start to finish.

Karl has established Sporting Clubs in Solihull, Sheffield, Bristol, Derby, Wolverhampton, Cheltenham, Sutton Coldfield, Warwick, Droitwich and Gloucester. So popular are the events that all Karl Ward's Sporting Club memberships are sold out. Ring him on 07000 527592 if you wish to be included on his membership waiting list.

David Duckham has also established a successful set of Sporting Clubs further South, between Stratford-Upon-Avon and the South Coast. For information, contact Southern Sporting Clubs, tel 01789 721621.

Luncheon Clubs

Mike Newlin (MBN Promotions) has established a number of extremely popular luncheon clubs throughout the country. The events usually follow a sporting theme, featuring some of the biggest sporting celebrities from the world of football, cricket, rugby, boxing, etc.

Although individual tickets are available, sponsored tables of 10 or 12 guests are the most popular, and there is one premier sponsorship package for a main sponsor. Sporting luncheons provide an ideal opportunity for companies wishing to entertain corporate clients 'within working hours'. Unlike evening functions, it is essential that Sporting Luncheons run exactly on time, to enable guests to return to their offices after the event.

MBN currently organise luncheons in Aberdeen, Belfast, Birmingham, Bristol, Cardiff, Chester, Dublin, Edinburgh, Glasgow, Leeds, Liverpool,

London, Manchester, Milton Keynes, Newcastle, Norwich, Nottingham, Preston and Stoke.

For information, see the MBN web site at: www.mbnpromotions.co.uk or telephone 0161 926 9569.

The Pub Dinner

Although most Sportsman's Dinners are held in hotels, clubs and large banqueting suites, they do sometimes take place in pubs. Many amateur football clubs have a local pub as their after-match watering hole (for some teams it is also the pre-match training ground), and landlords occasionally put on a Pub Dinner.

The average pub does not have a room large enough for a break-even attendance of 60-80 people. But a little ingenuity can make this smaller type of function profitable. It should be held on the quietest night of the week, usually Monday or Tuesday for public houses. Then any locals who pop in can be redirected to the snug for the evening.

The key to profitability is keeping costs down. That is, of course, unless the landlord wants to sponsor the evening to show his support for the team. If the cost of the meal can be kept low, and a Speaker can be persuaded to attend for free, even such a small attendance can provide an enjoyable and profitable night.

'A couple of years ago I was asked by a friend of my sons to speak at his Sportsman's Dinner at a pub in Rossendale. They were attempting to raise funds to buy new kit and could not afford any Speaker fees, so the event became one of my annual dozen or so charity nights.

When I arrived at around 7.30pm the team had started their training at the bar and a lively atmosphere was in the making. They obviously had a great affinity with the pub and the landlord, who wore a dinner jacket and was Master of Ceremonies for the night.

I counted 47 chairs packed into the lounge, but strangely there were no knives, forks and spoons, as you would expect. As I was enjoying a soft drink at the bar and chatting to the club secretary, he asked me if I liked chicken curry. "I hope so," he said, "because that's what we have ordered for you, with fried rice."

Ten minutes later the "kit man" arrived with two large binliners containing various take-away meals from the Chinese across the street. As our sweet course we all enjoyed a choc-ice from the newsagents next door. Then on to the speeches. The club captain was first on his feet, and he did well under the barrage of abuse he received from his teammates. My speech followed the Stand-Up Bingo, and a raffle and short auction ended the night's formalities. I said my good-byes at around 11.30pm and I think the rest of the team left the pub at about 12.00pm .... the following day.

Overall it was an enjoyable, and profitable, event. I rang my drinking partner the club secretary the following week to ask if they had made any money. He shared with me the following figures.

Tickets sold – 46 x £20.00	£920.00
48 takeaways @ discount price £4.95	(237.60)
48 choc ices @ 40p	(19.20)
Speaker	0.00
Compere	0.00
Stand-Up Bingo	92.50
Profit from raffle	240.00
Profit from auction	75.00
	————
Profit on the night	£1070.70

The club made a profit of over £1000 and I imagine that the bar takings were around the £500 mark. Not exactly the Waldorf, but it was nice to get back to grass-roots.'

22
The Testimonial Dinner

When professional sportsmen and sportswomen are granted a testimonial, it is usually in recognition of their exceptional service to a club, or because they have had to retire prematurely through serious injury.

Most professional sporting organisations (football, cricket, rugby, etc) give guidelines to the player on how a testimonial should be conducted. These usually require the player to ask a testimonial committee to stage events on his or her behalf. The player cannot be included on that committee, neither can directors or employees of his or her club. The committee has to appoint a Secretary and Treasurer and keep accurate records of both expenditure and minutes of their meetings.

Some sporting organisations recommend that their players seek confirmation from the appropriate Inspector of Taxes that the proceeds from their events are free from tax, and also recommend that the committee confine its activities to events such as matches and dinners. The greater the level of 'business activity', eg the sale of souvenirs, etc, the greater the chance of the Inspector of Taxes taking an interest. And if the turnover of the committee is likely to exceed the VAT threshold, currently £50,000 (early 1999), registration would be necessary. Anyone who is considering a testimonial should certainly seek professional, taxation and legal advice before they start.

Once a testimonial is set up, the Testimonial Dinner can be extremely profitable.

'In 1980, I was in the process of being transferred from Blackpool to Portsmouth, and if Alan Ball (the Blackpool manager) had not rung me to ask if I would play for Blackpool for "one last match" before my transfer, I might be living in Portsmouth today. What I did not know was that my last match for Blackpool would also double up as my last match in a 16-year career. After an innocent collision with their goalkeeper, my right leg was broken in two places and my ankle in three.

So, in late 1980 my testimonial committee organised on my behalf a Sportsman's Dinner with guest Speaker George Best and Comedian Frank Carson. It was an unnerving experience sitting at the top table in front of 300 paying guests and wondering if George would turn up. The daily papers had carried a few stories that week about George's drink problem and his non-appearance at functions.

The knot in my stomach quickly departed as George walked through the door of the Astoria Ballroom, Rawtenstall to the type of standing ovation reserved only for superstar geniuses. The evening was a great success and George was a perfect gentleman. His speech was superb and he sipped orange juice all night. Following the function, he stayed to sign autographs and chat to the mass of people who stayed behind to reminisce over old goals and old girlfriends. There is a certain aura around people who have been blessed with a rare talent, and many people still feel that George Best retired too early and deprived them of years of wonderful football entertainment.

The evening concluded late, and as my testimonial committee counted the money George's entourage took him back home to Manchester, with his fee in their pockets. It came as quite a shock when, two weeks later, a bill arrived from George's agent which was equivalent to twice the fee he had been paid on the night. It contained such items as:

First-class train tickets from Scotland

Hotel accommodation in Manchester for numerous people

Telephone calls to America

Six bottles of Champagne

Air tickets to Belfast

Taxis

Petrol bills, etc.

My testimonial chairman, Colin Waldron, a good friend and ex-Burnley team-mate, who himself had a spell as a Manchester United player, read out the invoice at my next Testimonial Committee meeting. He then said, "I suggest we rip it into pieces, throw it in the bin, and wait to see if we hear from them." To date we have heard nothing!'

There are several thngs that the recipient of a Testimonial Dinner can do to enhance the evening. For example:

* He can be held back and be seen for the first time as he is welcomed to the top table with the Guest of Honour and Celebrity Speakers.
* He can say Grace, draw the raffle, bingo and lucky draw, and propose the Loyal Toast.
* Most of all he must retain a certain distance and dignity, to encourage the evening's guests to 'put money into his bank account'.

> 'In 1994 I attended a Rugby League player's Testimonial Dinner. The player being rewarded arrived late and walked to the top table during the main course, in an open-necked shirt. Some members of the audience started to applaud quietly as he stumbled on to the stage, but most people heard him shout to his committee members, "Come on, Billy, let's get this crap out of the way and get down to the boozer."
>
> His contempt for his audience, supporters and top table guests poisoned the night. The evening never recovered. The other Speaker (an international cricketer) and I performed with mediocrity. The raffle flopped, as did the auction at which an autographed Wigan Rugby League Club ball sold for £15.
>
> Unfortunately the player being honoured that evening did not have the intelligence to assess the devastating impact his actions had on the fund-raising opportunities. Not only for that event, but for other dinners that would follow.'

At the end of the evening it is important for the recipient of a testimonial event to say a few words of thanks. This does not need to be an epic performance, just a sincere thank-you to show that he is grateful for both his testimonial committee's efforts and his audience's generosity.

Many recipients shy away from saying a few words of thanks, but if they really want the event to be successful, and make good money, they should be prepared to make a short speech. This can be something along the lines of:

'It's nice that I can have this opportunity to say thank-you to every one of you who has helped to make this evening so special for me. I will not try to thank each individual in the sure knowledge that I will miss someone out, but it is extremely rewarding that you have made such an effort to be here this evening and honour me in this way.

'I have been both fortunate and privileged to play professional (sport) for so many years, and my good fortune continued when I joined (club). I hope, when I look back in many years from now, that I will be satisfied that I gave sufficient dedication to my professional career, and now intend to have similar success in my future years.

'With the support you have shown tonight, I am confident that whatever I choose to do, my rewards will be equivalent to the work I put in. My sincere thanks to everyone.'

Alternatively, he can settle for something like this:

'Oh hell, I thought I might have to say sommat so I've had a few pints, ha ha ha ha. So here goes .... Unaccustomed as I am to public speaking ... ha ha ha ha.

'Now, who've I got to thank. Oh yes, the caterers for a lovely spread, thank you the committee for organising this for me, and my mum and dad for having me ... ha ha. And for all of you lot for coming tonight. And finally my Uncle Bill who wants to come up on stage and sing "Moon River". Let's have a big round of applause for Uncle Bill .... See you all at the bar later.'

Which would you choose?

23
The Schools Dinner

Over the last few years a new type of fund-raising function has started to emerge on the circuit. Now that schools and colleges are needing to be more commercial and are investigating every area of potential profitability, the Sporting Dinner is being adopted as an ideal vehicle to swell school funds. Schools also have the six main ingredients to make Sporting Dinners profitable.

1   The Need – to raise funds for the school
2   The Venue – most schools have a large assembly room
3   The Catering – on site and provided at cost
4   Car Parking – plenty if you include the playground
5   Ticket Sellers – the PTA or teachers with commercial ability
6   Ticket Sales Potential – every parent of every pupil.

Most of these functions are 'Sporting' (mixed) Dinners and often can become great community events. Whereas organising the event is relatively straightforward, the most difficult task is selling the tickets. However, this can be quite simple if it is attacked on three different fronts.

Firstly, the PTA can agree to take on this task. If ten members sell ten tickets each, the evening is immediately into profit (provided, of course, that the ticket price is budgeted to include a profit).

Secondly, the pupils can be asked to take a leaflet home, which explains the function and includes a tear-off slip for parents to apply for tickets.

Thirdly, there is a letter from the Head Teacher. This is carefully worded so that its target readers clearly understand the essential message, which is: ' to help little Johnny's education, buy two tickets for the Sporting Dinner'. The letter can also have a little fund-raiser built into the PS. (I do not know many other letters selling tickets where you could get away with this.) Below is an example of the type of letter that would get results. Each letter should be mail-merged by computer and personally signed in blue ink by the Head Teacher, preferably with first name only (though this is not always appropriate).

Sample Letter

Mr Dougie Doings
address and
postcode

Dear Dougie

As you know, we are striving hard at DD School to achieve a high standard of education for all our pupils, while under a cloud of constant cutbacks. But rather than let standards fall, we intend to have a series of fund-raising initiatives to raise funds for the school. This will allow us to maintain the standard of education in which we pride ourselves. To this aim I write to ask if you will support our first initiative.

On 23 April we are holding a Sporting Dinner at the School. The function starts at 7.30pm and ends no later than 11.30pm. The guest Speaker is Dougie Doings, an international cricketer, and there will also be a Comedian and professional Compere, yet to be announced. A three-course meal will be prepared by our own catering staff, and a bar, operated by the PTA, will be licensed up until 12 midnight.

Tickets are £17.50 each; £30 for a couple or £250 for a sponsored table of 10 should your company wish to entertain guests at the event. We also intend to have a raffle and a few fund-raisers as the evening unfolds.

I hope that you are able to support this function in the certain knowledge that all funds will go directly to the school, and I look forward to seeing you on the night.

Yours sincerely

Dougie   (personally signed in blue ink)

Dougie Doings
Headmaster

PS. I have included two tickets for you and Mrs Doings in the hope that, if you are not able to attend, you will still support the function by buying one or both of the tickets. Please return the tickets if you are not coming so that we can assess the numbers attending. Alternatively – you may wish to sponsor or donate a raffle prize?

Make a list of every person mailed, and for best results the Head Teacher should personally telephone everyone who does not respond after 7 days.

By following the guidelines set out in this book, the function should be relatively easy to organise. Make sure you book a big-name but not-too-costly Speaker for your first event to ensure you sell all the tickets. A good Agent will advise you on a suitable Speaker within your budget. You should also have a Comedian and a Compere.

After the event, retain your checklist, budget, running order and attendance list and you have a ready-made event for next year. And the year after, and the year after that.

Bloxham School
Under the banner 'Bloxham Sporting Club', many very successful dinners have been organised at Bloxham School, near Banbury. The dinners are held twice a year and in recent years have attracted such stars as Sir Stanley Matthews, Graham Gooch, Denis Law, David Lloyd, Willie John McBride and Nat Lofthouse, to name but a few.

Attendance is limited to 210 people in the Great Hall at Bloxham School, with the cost per dinner ranging around £30-35 per head. Although the events are run via the Bloxham Sporting Club, unlike many similar sporting clubs no annual fee is required.

During the evening there is a single fund-raising event, usually involving around £5 per head from all attending, with donations going to many local charities after the Dinner.

The aims of the Sporting Club are not commercially driven and are clearly stated on their publicity brochure. They are:

1   To provide an arena for corporate hospitality and entertaining.
2   To attract International Speakers to North Oxfordshire.
3   To raise money for charities and worthy local causes.

The dinners are now very well established, they sell out on each occasion and are an excellent example of how a Sporting Dinner can work well at a school. Anyone interested in being included on the mailing list is asked to write to Ian Slogan, c/o Bankier Sloan, Centrepoint, Chapel Square, Deddington, OX15 0SG.

Your First Dinner – the Potential

While writing this book, I was visited by Rick Wilson, the brother of a friend of mine, who inquired about fund-raising for his local junior boys' and girls' football teams. (Rick's brother Derek is an architect who has worked on the McAlpine Stadium, Reebok Stadium and Sydney 2000 Stadium.) One hour later he left my home with a badly photocopied draft copy of this book. Apart from a few phone calls and a couple of letters asking for clarification and contact numbers, he followed much of the advice contained within these pages. Below, in Rick's words, is a brief summary of the first dinner for a junior football team in a small village in West Yorkshire.

'Colts and Fillies Junior Football Club has been going since 1991, enhancing kids' participation in an enjoyable environment. I've been involved with the club over the last two years helping to coach the youngsters, and only in the last year have been involved in off-the-field events.

Derek put me in touch with Paul, and in March '98 we discussed the various options for fund-raising and eventually talked about a Sportsman's Dinner. As I had only the slightest idea of how to organise a dinner, I was literally diving into Paul's years of experience.

He showed me the draft of the book he was writing, and told me to go away and read it, which in turn would help me to set up and organise a successful Sportsman's Dinner from start to finish.

From the very first page, I realised we needed to adopt a true professional approach if we wanted everything to go smoothly.

The club's committee were very positive about the dinner. The secretary, chairman and I checked out the different venues in the town and after discussion with the owners and management of Scaitcliffe Hall, it was decided this venue would be ideal.

The date was set: Tuesday 2 June 1998.

Colts and Fillies Inaugural Sportman's Dinner

Over the next couple of months, the book was to prove an invaluable source of information with everything from the correct choice of food on the evening to the friendly sale of sponsorship technique.

We approached numerous local businesses regarding sponsorship on the evening and for the future, both in person (informally) and by letter (formally). The response was fantastic – everybody from large business companies to the small corner shops was keen to be involved.

Team managers and coaches and Mums were selling tickets like hot cakes, and with a week to go the night was a 135-seater sell-out.

The whole evening was a great success, especially seeing celebrity guests speaking in our local village, it certainly brought the whole community together that night. Bank managers sat next to butchers, smaller businesses were able to entertain customers and even our local Mayor, with gold chain of office, added greatly to the evening with his formal presence on the top table.

Right from day one, we were extremely optimistic and budgeted to make around £1500 profit.

Below is a summary of the evening's accounts.

Dinner – Date Tuesday 2 June 1998
Venue – Local Hotel
Attendance – 135
Cost of Ticket – £20

INCOME

Sponsorship	£1630.00
(includes tickets for some sponsored tables)	
Ticket sales (individual tickets)	2500.00
Raffle profit	559.00
Auction profit	360.00
Stand Up Bingo profit	540.00
	£5,589.00

EXPENDITURE

Meal and wine	£1499.00
(food @ £12 per head, some free)	
Entertainers	700.00
Sponsors' gifts	55.00
Programme print	56.40
Tickets print	22.00
Misc expenses	42.98
	————
	£2375.38
Total profit for event	£3213.62

Needless to say, the club intend to make this an annual event. The funds raised at the inaugural dinner will be extremely important in establishing junior boys' and girls' football in the village.'

24
Additional Entertainers

Many organisers who have been running Sportman's Dinners for many years are now looking to change the format and introduce something 'a little different'. It is very important constantly to seek to improve functions, and there are some agencies that specialise in providing 'alternative' types of act. If you are looking for something a little different, here are a few ideas.

Conjurer or Magician

People like to see card tricks, and magicians are now becoming very popular at Sportman's Dinners. It is quite easy for an experienced magician to walk amongst the guests during the meal and entertain them a table at a time. I once organised a dinner and the next day someone rang me to say, 'I thought the Speakers were good but the magician was magnificent.' I had paid the Speakers £500 each and the magician £75.

Jazz Band, Trio or Quartet

To give an evening a bit of sparkle, do not be afraid to book some musicians. Two spots are often a good idea, with the first between 7.30 and 8.00pm, on main reception, to welcome your guests. The second session could be a background to the main course, which gives plenty of time for them to be away before the main Speakers get to the microphone.

'In 1991 I spoke at one of the most enjoyable dinners I have ever had the pleasure of attending. I was booked along with David Howes, from the world of Rugby League, and the Compere was the magnificent Neil Midgley, ex-FIFA referee.

After struggling for 30 minutes to try and find the venue, I met Neil on the car park; he had also had difficulty finding the place. We both went cold when we saw the 'Palladium' ... a mission hut in deep East Lancashire.

When we walked in, it got worse. The school band were up on stage being conducted by a 60-year-old male conductor with purple hair, and a purple scarf to match (you know the sort). The vicar's wife met us at the front door of the hut to say that the food was being cooked by all the mothers, and all the boys and girls were serving us drinks. She gave us our free tombola ticket, showed us to the top table and said she hated football but loved cricket, and was delighted to meet "Test Match referee" Mr Midgley, and would we like a glass of fruit punch.

The vicar's wife continued, "I've sat you both between my husband, the vicar, and his friend Herbert, who is the vicar from the next parish, and DD who's our local reporter and my Uncle Albert who is 83 and deaf. I hope you have a lovely evening."

We sat in school chairs, with school plates and school glasses on school tables. The 85 people in the audience seemed friendly enough and quite relaxed; the school dinner arrived and was OK. The audience's good behavior was obviously due to the fact that their wives and children were serving them. We wondered if we had been invited to a Sportman's Dinner, a wake or a school assembly. Once the school meal had ended, the school band packed away, the wives and children said their goodbyes ... and the atmosphere completely changed. Within an hour, Neil Midgley, David Howes and I were the only ones still sober. The two vicars led the charge and the wine flowed like water. It was like an American speakeasy during Prohibition. The place was buzzing. Wine, whisky, brandy, Champagne, Southern Comfort, you name it, they drank it ... and that was only the two vicars. Neil Midgley relished the magnetic atmosphere, taking a rise out of the two inebriated vicars with such aplomb that both David Howes and I began to ache with laughter. Even Uncle Albert came in for some stick from "Midge" who always excels in these situations. When Neil Midgley is on form, he is hard to match.

It is nights like these, when unexpectedly the evening becomes more of a pleasure than a job, that after-dinner speaking can be one of the most rewarding experiences.'

Barber's Shop Quartet

Someone once said, 'There is no finer sound than four men singing in harmony', and I am sure they were right. Most towns have Barber's Shop Quartets or Choruses and many will be pleased to attend and sing for their supper.

The Mad Waiter

Believe it or not, it is now possible to book a professional mad waiter who will either act out a 'Mañuel' role from Fawlty Towers (but mix in with the rest of the waiters and waitresses), or work up a sequence to target one of the guests. Both are a little risky, but if judged correctly can provide excellent impromptu entertainment.

Crowd Pullers

For an insight into all the possible options for Additional Entertainers, there is a company called Crowd Pullers, based in London, who have a complete list of their entertainers. Their telephone number is 0181 305 0074.

25
What About Equality?

This book concentrates on Sportsman's Dinners. As I explained at the beginning, however, in the last few years more and more women have been attending this type of function, and gone are the days when a Speaker or Comedian would refuse to perform if women were in the room, or, alternatively, would ask the women to leave.

A mixed dinner can be an excellent evening and I have spoken at many such functions, including a number of Schools Dinners (see Section 23). But although the mixed Schools Dinner can make a healthy profit, particularly when all the members of the PTA – both Mums and Dads – are out there selling tickets to their friends, the revenue they generate is not on the same scale as that of the traditional Sportsman's Dinner. There are some straightforward reasons why this should be so.

*   Rarely will a company or Sponsor buy a table and invite along customers and their wives. Although it is an accepted business expense to entertain customers in an attempt to attract business, the addition of wives makes the event more social than business.

*   Tickets for mixed events often need to be sold on an individual basis, where a man is approached to buy tickets for himself and his wife (or vice versa). This will normally rule out a company sponsoring a table, so individuals have to pay for themselves.

*   Therefore, a man wishing to take his wife along will have to purchase a ticket for both of them, doubling his expenditure on tickets alone. When the fund-raiser comes along, the man will often buy raffle tickets 'between them' or on behalf of his wife. This either doubles his cost or halves the profit for the organisers.

*   Speakers and Comedians rarely perform as well in front of a mixed audience. Most sporting Speakers would never swear or use 'industrial language' in front of women, purely out of courtesy. But often a sporting anecdote, told straight from the heat of the contest, needs the odd expletive to make the story humorous. Although I have heard many women at functions say, 'Don't worry, I've heard it all before', this does not help the 'Gentlemen Speakers' or 'true Gentlemen' in the room who do not like to hear bad language in women's company.

*   Finally, there is the auction. This often raises far more than its true value. On many occasions I have seen autographed footballs, worth around £20, sell for more than £1000 at auction. I have often wondered if the bidder would have been quite so generous if he had had his wife sitting next to him.

Organisers sometimes arrange a mixed dinner in an attempt to break the all-male domain and sell tickets to the corporate business sector. The concept is to invite customers, both male and female, but neither can bring along a wife or husband. To keep the evening strictly on a business, not social, footing, guests can include a secretary, male or female, a work colleague or client. These functions are rarely successful, and often invited guests get in more hot water with their respective partners than the event is worth.

To sum up, the Sportsman's Dinner has evolved as a male domain. Market forces have made all-male dinners far more profitable than mixed events. But as we approach the millennium and times quickly change, I am sure the concept of fund-raising dinners will also change as many women are now themselves becoming 'Captains of Industry'. They will then spend their sponsorship or entertainment budget in line with their company's needs. I am confident that it will not be long before the mixed function is equally as profitable as the all-male event.

To give a balanced view, it must also be said that there are many Ladies' Dinner Clubs up and down the country. Not very long ago I was guest

Speaker at the Barrowford Ladies' Dinner Club, and it was an excellent event.

Women Speakers

There are quite a few excellent female Speakers and Comedians on the circuit. Many attend all-male evenings and are very familiar with how to entertain such audiences. Often these ladies feel more comfortable with an all-male audience and are able to entertain just as well as the men.

Entertainers with Disabilities

It would be remiss of me not to mention the entertainers on the circuit who have various forms of disability. I have worked alongside Speakers and Comedians who are either blind, on crutches, sit in wheelchairs or have arms and legs missing.

Believe me, these guys are not looking for the sympathy laugh, and rarely do they get it. They get booked for dinners for one simple reason ... they have the ability to entertain. And sometimes they can really relax the audience by poking fun at themselves.

IOT
Do not worry about booking a Speaker or Comedian who
is disabled. If they have survived the circuit, it means they
are talented.

26
Corporate Entertainment

There are various types of corporate entertainment. This section concentrates specifically on the Sporting Dinner. Corporate entertainment is probably the most precise marketing tool currently available. It helps you to forge and strengthen relationships with people who are important to the success of your business. Those people could be customers or employees, potential customers or members of various organisations associated with your company. Irrespective of who they are, you need to get to know them better; more importantly, they need to get to know you better.

Corporate entertainment works – as long as you do it right.

All over the country, business people are coming to realise the importance of corporate entertaining. They are learning to appreciate the importance of human relationships within the role of business.

Companies now study carefully how they win new business through personal contact. In the past they would analyse how to motivate their staff to stay with them and achieve better results, or how to create more effective direct-marketing campaigns. Now they evaluate what they want to achieve through their business relationships, and an evening socialising at a Sporting Dinner can often be a cost-effective investment.

Instead of simply inviting a customer out to dinner and pouring as much drink as possible down their throat, the more far-sighted companies are now planning their dinner strategy with the same amount of care as they give to their advertising and direct-mail campaigns.

Who sits with who, the wine, the company gift, overnight accommodation, flowers to take home to the wives, free raffle tickets, meet the celebrities, the follow-up letter or the phone call. The list is endless. But it needs to be planned precisely for the best results.

Sales & Marketing is simply a concept for moving people through from a position where they do not know anything about you to knowing who you are, liking and trusting you, purchasing from you and then continuing to purchase from you. Without doubt it is always better to do business with friends than strangers.

Even professionals such as bankers, accountants and solicitors can succeed or fail according to the quality of the relationships they manage to build with their clients. Advertisements or inquiries could be a starting point in their marketing campaign, but it is more likely to be through corporate entertaining and human relationships, or their success in 'networking', that they reap the real rewards.

Once this relationship has been established, the number one purchasing consideration, price, can become secondary. It is said that if the price was the only consideration there would only be one car manufacturer, one pen manufacturer, one shirt manufacturer, and so on. But other issues come into the buying process and, make no mistake, personal relationships come very high on the agenda. As Confucius said, 'Man with sad face shouldn't open shop.'

Many companies now have some form of customer care programme. One of the main aims of this strategy is to generate customer loyalty. Companies take increasing care over customers who come back and complain. Without doubt, the way a complaint is handled could cement a lifetime relationship. On the other hand, treat your customer's complaint badly and you wave them goodbye forever.

Every penny spent on building relationships and goodwill within your business is a legitimate business expense, and should be included in the budget just as formally as the money that is going into an advertising or direct-marketing campaign.

I once read that 'The only selling effort that is deemed more effective than corporate hospitality is the use of the direct sales force.' It is a powerful statement and comes directly from someone who has tried it and knows that it works. The only problem with using the Sportsman's Dinner as a form of corporate entertainment arises if corporate hosts do not have a clear understanding of exactly what they are doing. They may simply think it is a good idea, so then they find the necessary budget to proceed. But often they do not have a clear brief.

Although the evening itself may be judged a success, most companies do not realise what a wonderful opportunity it is to use the Sportsman's Dinner as a precise marketing tool. Even making a small investment in researching their invited guests can provide significant results, especially if the research is based on non-business activities.

A Sportsman's Dinner is not an opportunity to conduct business across the table. It is an opportunity to put the balance sheet away and talk to your customers about everything but business. This is a forum for common subjects such as holidays, children, football teams, food, wine and music. So, if you want to make a real friend of your best customer, find out what interests him. What is his hot button? This is where your research comes in. And you will be amazed what you will uncover. It might be pottery, painting, hang-gliding, trainspotting, Henry VIII, deep-sea diving or Elvis Presley. Find out a few interesting questions, talk to him about this subject, be genuinely interested ... and you will have a friend for life.

It can continue to be a bond between you throughout your business relationship. Once you have found the right button to press, do not be scared to press it. A newspaper cutting, postcard, photograph, book, model, brochure, article, exhibition – you will find endless opportunities to fan the flame. That is, of course, if you believe in this concept. Dale Carnegie once wrote in his famous book, *How to Win Friends and Influence People*: 'The best way to be an interesting conversationalist is to find out what interests your guest, and then sit and listen to him.'

Newspaper Advertising

You could of course use your valuable sales and marketing budget on various other methods of attracting more business for your company. A newspaper advertisement may cost around the same as a table for ten at a Sportsman's Dinner. It could be read by many thousands of potential customers. But three weeks later you may find the advertisement has made no difference to your sales or level of inquiries.

However, if you can get ten good prospects to the right place at the right time you immediately have ten strong leads. What is more, if you meet up in a social environment initially, this makes the business side far more relaxed, as by this time you are not talking to a cold customer.

Executive Boxes

Over the past twenty years corporate hospitality around sporting events has grown into a multi-million pound business. Football in particular has benefited from the executive box, or hospitality suite as it is called at some grounds. The concept is very simple. Ten people gathered together in a room measuring around 3m x 4m for 5 to 6 hours. They enjoy good car parking, hospitality hostesses, free match programmes, super food, excellent wine – a quality environment. Oh, and by the way, at 3pm there is a football match going on in the green field through the glass. Often the match can be a distraction to a good day out!

Many companies who have national accounts plan their guest list for every match many weeks before the season kicks off. They simply select business associates who are supporters of the visiting club. This gives the afternoon an added sparkle. Two hosts, who are selling a product, represent the home club, and eight guests, who are buying a product, represent the away club. Irrespective of the result, the banter throughout the afternoon provides enough to talk about for the next twelve months – or until the next match.

Where Are the Best Prospects?

Without doubt, they are already there, waiting within an existing customer base. The most difficult part is always the first sale. After that it is simply a matter of building upon what you have established. In many companies, the old cliché that 80 per cent of business comes from 20 per cent of customers is consistently true.

Beware of the Queue

Because so many companies are recognising the value of corporate entertainment, many of their intended guests turn down more invitations to Sportsman's Dinners than they accept. The more important the individuals are, the harder it will be for you to tempt them away from their desks, or their homes, to be with you.

The hardest part can often be getting RSVPs. This kind of entertaining has gone past the stage of sending a simple invitation letter with a reply-paid envelope. Nowadays the invitation process is more complex, and the event will need to be sold well in advance. For a Sportsman's Dinner, an acceptable invitation period is six to eight weeks prior to the event. There is another ratio to work to: 'The more important your guest, the longer the invitation period'. Or, to put it another way, 'Do not ask an important guest two weeks before the evening'. He will either think your planning is awful or, even worse, that you have asked everyone else and he is the last on the list. Do not risk the insult. If you have left it too late, put your next-door neighbour in the empty seat. There is always a next time.

A couple of days prior to the event, do not forget to make one last personal call to check that your guests are all happy with the itinerary. You can make arrangements to get them picked up, dropped off, overnight accommodation, taxis, etc. This last-minute attention to detail will confirm to your guest that you really want him to be there, and makes it harder for him to let you down.

Here is a good planning strategy that works (see also Section 16, 'Sponsorship'):

1   Book a table for 10 people.

2   List below 12 guests you would like to invite.

1) Yourself	Tel	9)	Tel
2)	Tel	10)	Tel
3)	Tel	11)	Tel
4)	Tel	12)	Tel
5)	Tel	13)	Tel
6)	Tel	14)	Tel
7)	Tel	15)	Tel
8)	Tel	16)	Tel

Also list four reserves, just in case.

3   Ring them personally to invite them (you will have far more success this way than asking your secretary to ring, or writing an invitation). Give yourself two days to complete the task.

4   Write confirming their attendance saying that you will forward the tickets and detailed arrangements nearer to the function date.

5   Remember that this is a planned corporate entertainment strategy intended to create more business for your company, and that your guests will welcome any additional attention to detail. Remind yourself to:

    *   Get there early and meet them at reception
    *   Prepare a table plan and use place cards
    *   Consider a small gift

*   Pre-order wine – arrange a bar account
*   Find out if overnight accommodation is needed for any guests
*   After the function, write and thank them for attending.

Remember these words: 'A guest never forgets a host who treats him kindly.' Homer.

It is always far easier to do business with personal friends than with business associates. What better, more cost-effective way can there be to entertain your guests than at a Sportsman's Dinner?

To sum up, corporate entertaining at a Sportsman's Dinner can be an excellent way of increasing your company's business. And, for the best results, make sure you pre-plan your strategy and give yourself plenty of time to carry it out.

27
The Day After

WHAT A NIGHT! The sound of the laughter is still ringing in your ears. Although you have a thick head and you got to bed late, there is still a sense of satisfaction and relief that the night went so well. At 9.30am, the proceeds will be paid into the club's bank account and life can get back to normal, until next year. All the hard work is over.

But wait a minute. There is still a lot of work to be done to prepare for next year's event. Do not let the opportunity go by without saying a big thank-you to everyone who has helped to contribute to your dinner. This simple gesture will not only be welcomed by the recipient, it will open the door for you to ask their help next year. Remember the law of selling: 'Spend 50 per cent of your time asking and 50 per cent of your time saying thank you.'

Thank-you Time

Who is there to thank? Well, here is a list of possibilities from among your:

>Sponsors
>Guest of Honour
>Committee Members
>Guest Speakers, Compere and Comedian
>Caterers
>Hotel
>Agents
>Anyone who donated a prize
>Local Newspaper that covered the event
>Raffle Ticket Sellers
>Printers
>Car Park Attendants
>Everyone who entered the Business Card Draw.

And how about a bunch of flowers for your wife for putting up with you over the past few weeks?

Keep a database of those valuable names and addresses if you want to call on the same team next year. For the next nine months you can keep your ears open for other Speakers and a different Comedian. If your Compere performed well, pencil him in for next year – if he is so good he might get booked up quickly.

File away in a safe place last night's menu/programme, running order, profit-and-loss account, budget, checklist, etc. They will all come in handy next year.

Well done. Now life can get back to normal. Er ... what was that joke about the Irishman?

Part Six

APPENDICES

Appendix I: Competitions

Fast-changing World

Before you use any of these sporting questions, here is a point to ponder. Einstein once set the same exam paper for two consecutive years. When questioned about his error, he replied: *'I have set the same questions because since last year the answers have changed.'*

We live in a quickly changing world so it might be a good idea to check a few of the answers to the sporting questions to see if they are still correct.

Answers are shown in italics, and correct answers to multiple-choice questions are shown in bold type.

GOT A SPARE POUND IN YOUR POCKET?

Complete the following and hope to win a few more.

Name the England side beaten by Brazil 1-0 in 1978. The first letter of each player's surname is provided.
The person with the most correct names will be declared the winner and can collect his prize from our guest of the evening.
Just place your selection with your £1.00 in the envelope provided – and do not forget your name! We will collect them from your table and the panel will declare the winner.

Team

C ... (orrigan)

S... (ansom)   G... (reenoff)   W... (atson)   C... (herry)

C... (urrie)   K.... (eegan)

C... (oppell)   L... (atchford)   L... (ee)   B... (arnes)

Your Name ....   **Table No** ....

DREAM TEAM

Pick Your Own Dream Team

£2.00 per team – £5.00 for 3 teams

Winning team to be selected by tonight's guest.

1	A	Schmeichel	B	Seaman	C	Martyn
2	A	G Neville	B	Petrescu	C	McAteer
3	A	Le Saux	B	P Neville	C	Bjornebye
4	A	Bilic	B	Leboeuf	C	Hendry
5	A	Southgate	B	Campbell	C	Ehiogu
6	A	Keane	B	Ince	C	Batty
7	A	Beckham	B	Le Tissier	C	McManaman
8	A	Viera	B	De Matteo	C	Redknapp
9	A	Shearer	B	Wright	C	Fowler
10	A	Sheringham	B	Zola	C	Bergkamp
11	A	Giggs	B	Wilcox	C	Ginola

	1	2	3	4	5	6	7	8	9	10	11
Team 1											
Team 2											
Team 3											

Your Name .... **Table No** ....

HOW WELL DO YOU KNOW YOUR CLUBS?

Most football clubs have a second name, for example, Leeds **UNITED**, Manchester **CITY**. We think there are 19 different **ENGLISH LEAGUE** names. Compile your list below.

1 .... UNITED

2 .... CITY

3 .... WANDERERS

4 .... ORIENT

5 .... ROVERS

6 .... VALE

7 .... ARGYLE

8 .... COUNTY

9 .... TOWN

10 .... NORTH END

11 .... RANGERS

12 .... VILLA

13 .... PALACE

14 .... WEDNESDAY

15 .... ATHLETIC

16 .... ALBION

17 .... HOTSPUR

18 .... ALEXANDRA

19 .... FOREST

£1 per entry

Your Name .... **Table No** ....

FOOTBALL QUIZ (1)

1   Which full back scored 10 goals in season 1969-70 for Liverpool?
     Chris Lawler

2   Who scored six hat-tricks in first division season 1960-61?
     Jimmy Greaves

3   Who holds the record number of appearances for Wales?
     Neville Southall

4   What English record is Pat Kruse (Torquay) not very proud of?
     Quickest own goal (6secs)

5   Has a player ever captained two World Cup sides?
     No

6   Who did England beat 17-0 in 1951?
     Australia

7   What is England's best placed finish in the European Championship and in what year?
     3rd – 1968

8   In what year did England players sing 'Back Home'?
     1970 – Mexico

9   What was unusual about the 2-2 draw between Aston Villa and Leicester in 1976?
     Chris Nichol scored all 4 goals

10   Who won the first League Cup Final at Wembley?
     QPR

11   Kevin Keegan's first three internationals were against the same country. Which one?
     Wales

12   Who succeeded Tommy Docherty as Scottish football manager in 1974?
     Willie Ormond

Your Name ....   **Table No** ....

FOOTBALL QUIZ (2)

1   Which Premiership club since 1920 has included seven England captains among its ranks and who are they? *Southampton (Keegan, Ball, Shilton, Channon, Wright, Mills, Watson)*

2   Which former North-East Football League clubs played at:
a) Holliday Park b) Portland Park c) The Paradise Ground?
Durham City, Ashington, Middlesborough, Ironopolis

3   Who was the last cricketer to achieve the double of 1,000 runs and 100 wickets in England? *Franklin Stevenson, 1988*

4   Name the first footballer to represent England while playing for a non-English club? *Joe Baker (Hibs), 1965*

5   Who is the oldest footballer to be capped for England since the war?
Les Compton, aged 38, in 1951

6   Name the smallest town in England to have a team in the old First Division?
Glossop

7   Name five Scottish League Clubs with grounds south of Berwick? *Stranraer, Queen of the South, Ayr United, Kilmarnock, Berwick Rangers (who play in Tweedmouth)*

8   Which three Sheffield Wednesday players were jailed for match-fixing in 1964?
Peter Swan, Tony Kay, David (Bronco) Lane

9   Only five Northern League champions since 1962-63 are still in the League.
Name them. *Evenwood, Billingham Synthonis, Durham City, Whitby Town, Tow Law*

10 Name five Premiership managers who have won FA Cup-winner's medals.
Bryan Robson (Man United), Kevin Keegan (Liverpool), Joe Kinnear (Spurs), Glen Hoddle (Spurs), Ray Wilkins (Man United)

11 If an entire cricket team is out first ball, what number is the not-out batsman?
Number Eight

12 Excluding angling, name four sports played with a net but no ball.
Badminton, Ice Hockey, Throwing the Hammer and Women's International Showjumping (where wearing a hairnet is compulsory)

13 Which record did Gordon Banks break in England's 5-0 win over Malta in 1971?
He touched the ball four times, all from back passes

14 What was missing from the 1959 FA Cup final, but present at every other final?
Abide with me

Your Name ....   **Table No** ....

QUESTIONNAIRE

You have two minutes to answer the following questions

1   Put the Prime Minister's name backwards in the square provided.*

2   Who has the 4th of July, USA or Britain?
    Both

3   A man built a rectangular house with each of the walls having a southern exposure. A bear came wandering past, what colour was the bear?
    White

4   Divide 30 by 1/2 and add 10.
    70

5   If you take two apples from three apples, what do you have?
    Two apples

6   You are in a room with no light at the dead of night. There is a candle, an oil lamp and a fire but you only have one match, which do you light first?
    Match

7   Some months have 31 days, some have 30. How many months have 28?
    12

8   You are driving a bus from Huddersfield carrying 40 passengers. You drive to the Jug & Bottle where 8 get off and 4 get on, proceeding to Bogey's. Here 12 get off and only 1 gets on, you then drive to The County for a right booze up. What is the drivers name?
    Your Name

    RIALB YNOT

Your Name ....   **Table No** ....

*Most people will write in the RECTANGLE at the top instead of the SQUARE at the bottom

JUST FOR FUN

In which season did the Football League Division Four cease to exist?
1991-1992

Which teams comprised the league?

1	*Burnley*	12	*Scarborough*
2	*Rotherham*	13	*Chesterfield*
3	*Mansfield*	14	*Wrexham*
4	*Blackpool*	15	*Walsall*
5	*Scunthorpe*	16	*Northampton*
6	*Crewe*	17	*Hereford*
7	*Barnet*	18	*York*
8	*Rochdale*	19	*Halifax*
9	*Cardiff*	20	*Doncaster*
10	*Lincoln*	21	*Carlisle*
11	*Gillingham*	22	*Maidstone*

And finally, whose record was expunged from that of that division during the season?
Maidstone

Your Name .... **Table No** ....

PICK THE TEAM

Select your best football team.
Pick one from each group of four (including three substitutes 12, 13 & 14) and make a second choice from each of the 14 groups.

1 a G Banks b P Jennings c P Shilton d D Seaman	6 a A Hansen b G Pallister c J Charlton d B Moore	11 a G Best b T Finney c D Anderton d S Matthews
2 a J Armfield b G Cohen c T Smith d G Neville	7 a A Ball b K Keegan c B Robson d J Barnes	12 a C Bell b M Hughes c P Madeley d L Ferdinand
3 a T Cooper b S Pearce c K Sansom d R Wilson	8 a K Dalglish b G Hurst c D Law d A Shearer	13 a N Lofthouse b J Greaves c L Dixon d D Wise
4 a P Gascoigne b D Blanchflower c B Bremner d G Souness	9 a F Lee b G Lineker c I Rush d T Sheringham	14 a R Giggs b T McDermott c R Kennedy d N Stiles
5 a T Butcher b M England c R McFarland d T Adams	10 a D Platt b L Brady c B Charlton d G Hoddle	

Number	1st Choice (A,B,C or D)	2nd Choice (A,B,C or D)	Number	1st Choice (A,B,C or D)	2nd Choice (A,B,C, or D)
1			8		
2			9		
3			10		
4			11		
5			12		
6			13		
7			14		
Total 1st 7			Total 2nd 7		

Your Name .... **Table No** ....

SPORTSMAN'S DINNER QUIZ

1   What is the length of a standard tennis court?
    A 74 ft   **B 78ft**   C 82ft

2   Which County Cricket Club has its Headquarters at Sophia Gardens?
    A Hampshire   **B Glamorgan**   C Gloucestershire

3   Which Welsh Rugby Union Club play in all black?
    A Neath   B Cardiff   C Swansea

4   Which Football Club plays its home games at Annfield Park?
    A Liverpool   B Airdrie   **C Stirling Albion**

5   What colour coat does the dog in Trap 1 in greyhound racing wear?
    A Red   B Black   C Blue

6   Who won the 1994 British Open Golf Championship?
    A Nick Price   B Greg Norman   C Nick Faldo

7   KMD is Kenny Dalglish's private number plate. What does the 'M' stand for?
    A Morgan   **B Matheson**   C Matius

8   Which country has won the most Olympic gold medals at Hockey?
    A Australia   B Pakistan   **C India**

9   Who knocked Lennox Lewis out at Wembley in September 1994?
    A Winston McCall   B Leroy McCall   **C Oliver McCall**

10 Who was the last Australian to win the Men's Single Title at Wimbledon?
    A John Newcombe   **B Pat Cash**   C Rod Laver

11 What do the initials W G stand for in W G Grace?
    A Wilfred Gilbert   **B William Gilbert** C William George

12 Where was the 1964 Olympic Games held?
    A Mexico   B Rome   **C Japan**

13 If a checkered flag is used to end a Grand Prix, what coloured flag is waved at the start of a Grand Prix?
    The colour of the country where it takes place

Your Name ....   **Table No** ....

WORLD CRICKET TEAM

Choose your post-war all-time great World Cricket XI from the following players.

Batsmen – Select any 5 (circle)

GEOFF BOYCOTT
DON BRADMAN
GREG CHAPPELL
DENIS COMPTON
COLIN COWDREY
MARTIN CROWE
SUNIL GAVASKAR
GRAHAM GOOCH
DAVID GOWER
NEIL HARVEY
LEN HUTTON
BRIAN LARA
BILL LAWRY
PETER MAY
HANIF MOHAMMAD
GRAEME POLLOCK
BARRY RICHARDS
VIV RICHARDS
BOB SIMPSON
EVERTON WEEKES

All-Rounders – Select 1 only

TREVOR BAILEY
RICHIE BENAUD
IMRAN KHAN
KEITH MILLER
CLIVE RICE
GARY SOBERS
STEVE WAUGH

Bowlers – Select any 4

CURTLEY AMBROSE
BISHEN BEDI
JOEL GARNER
LANCE GIBBS
MICHAEL HOLDING
JIM LAKER
DENNIS LILLEE
RAY LINDWALL
TONY LOCK
MICHAEL PROCTOR
ANDY ROBERTS
BRIAN STATHAM
FRED TRUEMAN
FRANK TYSON
SHANE WARNE

Wicket-keepers – Select 1 only

WASIM BARI
FAROKH ENGINEER
GODFREY EVANS
WALLY GROUT
IAN HEALEY
ALAN KNOTT
ROD MARSH
DON TALLON·
BOB TAYLOR
CLYDE WALCOTT

My Choice of 12th Man is:

....

Rules: In the event of a tie, the twelfth man will count
One entry only per competiton. The Umpire's decision is final.

Your Name ....   **Table No** ....

PICK YOUR SPORTING GREATS

			Entry 1	Entry 2

CRICKET
Bowler

A Tony Lock	B Jim Laker	C Harold Larwood	......	......

Wicket-keeper

A Godfrey Evans	B Alan Knott	C Deryk Murray	......	......

Batsman

A Geoff Boycott	B Viv Richards	C Gary Sobers	......	......

FOOTBALL
Goalkeeper

A Gordon Banks	B Frank Swift	C Peter Shilton	......	......

Player

A Tommy Smith	B Jimmy Greaves	C Nat Lofthouse	......	......

BOXING

A Bruce Woodcock	B Muhammad Ali	C Mike Tyson	......	......

HORSE RACING

A Lester Piggott	B Pat Eddery	C Gordon Richards	......	......

GOLF

A Seve Ballesteros	B Jack Nicklaus	C Arnold Palmer	......	......

ATHLETICS

A Steve Ovett	B Seb Coe	C Roger Bannister	......	......

RUGBY

A Ellery Hanley	B Billy Boston	C Alex Murphy	......	......

DARTS

A John Lowe	B Eric Bristow	C Jocky Wilson	......	......

£1 PER ENTRY

MAXIMUM 2 ENTRIES   PRIZE SHARED IF MORE THAN 1 WINNER

Your Name ....   **Table No** ....

FOOTBALL

Your Best World XI Since 1966.

1 .... (Goalkeeper)

2 ....

3 ....

4 ....

5 ....

6 ....

7 ....

8 ....

9 ....

10 ....

11 ....

12 ....

Subs

13 ....

14 ....

15 ....

16 .... (Goalkeeper)

Manager ....

Your Name ....   **Table No** ....

SPORTS QUIZ (1)

1   Which famous Golf Course has each of its 18 holes named after the flower, tree, shrub or bush that can be found adjacent to it?
Augusta

2   In which sport do participants compete for the Britannia Cup?
Rowing

3   With which sport do you associate the name Camp Freddie?
Sailing

4   Which professional Rugby League team are known as the Cougars?
Keighley

5   In cricket, the Lawrence Trophy is presented annually for what achievement?
The fastest first-class century

6   Who was selected Captain of the British Lions Tour to New Zealand in 1993?
Gavin Hastings

7   Who was Britain's only swimming medallist at the Barcelona Olympic Games?
Nick Gillingham

8   Apart from Brazil, which two countries have won the World Cup on three occasions or more?
Italy and West Germany

9   How old must thoroughbred horses be before they are allowed to race?
2 years

10 Name the winner of the 100 and 200 metres at the 1984 Olympic Games?
Carl Lewis

11 Who is the only Irishman to have won the British Open?
Fred Daly

12 Which famous Scottish International played for Torino in the early 1960s?
Denis Law

Your Name .... **Table No** ....

SPORTS QUIZ (2)

Only 12 players have captained England's soccer team more than 15 times.

Name them.

1 . . . . .Bobby Moore . . . .(90)

2 . . . . .Billy Wright . . . .(90)

3 . . . . .Bryan Robson . . . . . .(65)

4 . . . . .Kevin Keegan . . . .(29)

5 . . . . .Emlyn Hughes . . . . . .(24)

6 . . . . .Johnny Haynes . . . . .(22)

7 . . . . .Robert Crompton . . . .(21)

8 . . . . .Eddie Hapgood . . . . .(19)

9 . . . . .Gary Lineker . . . .(18)

10 . . . . .Jimmy Armfield . . . . .(15)

11 . . . . .Norman Bailey . . . . . .(15)

12 . . . . .Peter Shilton . . . .(15)

Your Name .... **Table No** ....

FOOTBALL JOURNEY

Insert the missing words below. All are English and Scottish football teams. Please note: the spellings may not be exact, but the dots represent the number of letters in the missing word (. . . / . . . . . . = two words)

The sun shone . . . . that . . . . morning when we set sail for the . . . . . . in a ship with a . . . . riddled with holes. One oar was loose until we put a . . . . . . the nut to tighten it. The Captain found his wife and we were all pleased to see the . . . / . . . . . . with his partner. We sailed down the river which . . . . . to the sea. We waved to a fair maiden leaning against the . . . . The . . . . . was made up of Scots, Irish and others of the . . . . . . race. The exception was the cabin boy named . . . . . whose job it was to . . . . . the boilers. He was illiterate but won our . . . . . . with his . . . . efforts to improve his . . . . He was sent to . . . . by other villains who had brought their . . . . of weapons on board. They were a rowdy lot and after a bout of drinking they did in fact . . . . furniture. The voyage made my . . . . as she had not had a holiday . . . . . . too long and the sea . . . did her . . . . lot of good. We landed . . . . . . in the day on the . . . . of the island, below where the natives . . . . their dead. We crossed a stream and a dense . . . . . . where the . . . . . . roamed freely. We . . . . regardless and eventually met a group of . . . . dressed in . . . . green. After a day's journey we caught some black fish in a . . . . and tried to get some milk from a herd of cows, but they did not like having their . . . . At last we came to our destination, the home of the Hawaiian monarch, the . . . . . / . . / . . . / . . . . . . She greeted us with a friendly . . . . . but was very upset as her . . . . / . . . . . had been smashed when the . . . . fell down. While her . . . . was being built, she had to live in a sumptuous . . . . . . When we found the treasure we put the . . . . . the ship, determined to put it in the . . . . when we got home. That night we had . . . . . . cake and . . . . buns for tea, and some . . . . . . which made us very ill.

Answers
Brighton, Wednesday, Orient, Hull, Bolton, Man United, Leeds, Millwall, Crewe, Celtic, Clyde, Stoke, Hearts, Sterling, Reading, Coventry, Arsenal, Wrexham, Motherwell, Forfar, Ayr, Chester, Leyton, Southend, Bury, Forest, Wolves, Preston, Rangers, Lincoln, Blackpool, Huddersfield, Queen of the South, Alloa, Crystal Palace, Walsall, Newcastle, Villa, Luton, Halifax, Dundee, Chelsea, Oldham.

Your Name . . . .   **Table No** . . . .

101 GREAT SPORTING QUESTIONS

1   Who succeeded Bob Paisley as Manager of Liverpool Football Club?
Joe Fagan

2   In which sport did Harry Mallin win 2 gold medals for Britain?
Boxing

3   Which golfer won the Open Championship in 1971 and 1972?
Lee Trevino

4   In which country did Muhammad Ali fight George Foreman in 1974?
Zaire

5   On which course did Nick Price win the 1994 British Open Golf title?
Turnberry

6   Which home Football Club would you see playing at Vicarage Road?
Watford

7   How many times did Bjorn Borg win the Wimbledon singles title?
5 times

8   With which team did Nigel Mansell win the world motor racing championship?
Williams-Renault

9   Who was the youngest member of England's 1996 World Cup squad?
Alan Ball

10   How many Olympic gold medals has rower Steve Redgrave won to date?
4

11   Which player captained West Indies in the 1996 Cricket World Cup?
Richie Richardson

12   Who coxed the Searle brothers to their gold medal in Barcelona?
Gerry Herbert

13   Who won the 1993 Badminton Horse Trials on Houdini?
Virginia Leng

14   Who managed Scotland's 1978 World Cup squad?
Aly MacLeod

15   With which sport do you associate the name Pedro Delgado?
Cycling

16   Which international football superstar is known as the Ice Man?
Dennis Bergkamp

17   What nationality is tennis star Gabriela Sabatini?
Argentinian

18   In which city do the Chargers play their home American Football matches?
      San Diego

19   Which gymnast was first in 1976 to be awarded a perfect mark 10?
      Nadia Comaneci

20   Who in 1996 became the first post-war player to score more than 30 goals in each of three successive seasons?
      Allan Shearer

21   In which year did Lynn Davies's long jump win an Olympic gold medal?
      1964

22   Which jockey rode Red Rum to his third Grand National victory?
      Tommy Stack

23   From which Italian club did Newcastle sign Faustino Asprilla?
      Parma

24   With which sport do you associate the name Judy Grinham?
      Swimming

25   Who were runners-up in the 1995-96 Coca Cola Cup Final?
      Leeds United

26   Who managed the 1982 England World Cup squad?
      Ron Greenwood

27   Who did Pat Cash beat in the 1987 Wimbledon men's singles final?
      Ivan Lendl

28   Who was Australia's leading wicket-taker in the 1994-95 Ashes series?
      Craig McDermott

29   Which boxer is nick-named the 'Atomic Bull'?
      Oliver McCall

30   Which Scottish club play their home matches at Brockville Park?
      Falkirk

31   With which club did Kevin Keegan start his Football League career?
      Scunthorpe United

32   Which former world heavyweight champion is nicknamed Real Deal?
      Evander Holyfield

33   Which pop star made the official choice of the best-looking player in the 1994 World Cup finals?
      Madonna

34   Who twice won the British Show Jumping Derby on Apollo?
      Nick Skelton

35   What nationality is Rugby Union legend Hugo Porta?
      Argentinian

36   Which West Indian fast bowler was nicknamed 'Big Bird'?
      Joel Garner

37   What nationality is snooker player Alain Robidoux?
      Canadian

38   With which sport do you associate the name Geoff Hunt?
      Squash

39   Who was the first cricketer to score a century and take 10 wickets in the same test?
      Ian Botham

40   Which country hosted the 1978 World Cup?
      Argentina

41   In which American City do the Rockets play basketball?
      Houston

42   From which club did Gary McAllister join Leeds?
      Leicester City

43   Who was signed by Chesterfield from Rawmarsh Welfare and went on to win a World Cup Winner's medal in 1966?
      Gordon Banks

44   How many times did Arnold Palmer win the Open Golf title?
      Twice

45   Who won the Olympic women's tennis singles title in 1992?
      Jennifer Capriati

46   What nationality is show-jumper Mark Todd?
      New Zealander

47   Of which England player did Ron Atkinson observe: 'The only time he goes forward is to toss the coin'?
      Ray Wilkins

48   Who changed his hair colour so many times that a toy manufacturer supplied paint for kids to touch up their models of him?
      Paul Gascoigne

49   On which ground did Geoff Boycott score his 100th first-class century?
      Headingley

50   With which team did Niki Lauda first win the world motor racing title?
      Ferrari

51   Who was the first England captain under Terry Venables?
      David Platt

52   At which weight was John H Stracey world boxing champion?
      Welterweight

53   Who scored the winning goal for Everton in the 1995 FA Cup Final?
      Paul Rideout

54   Who beat Ken Rosewall in straight sets in the 1974 Wimbledon singles final?
      Jimmy Connors

55   On which ground did Ian Botham score 149 not out in the 1981 Test series against Austrialia?
      Headingley

56   Against which country did John Barnes score his first goal for England?
      Brazil

57   Who was the first British golfer to win the US Open after the war?
      Tony Jacklin

58   Which club play their home football matches at Plainmoor?
      Torquay United

59   What nationality is Grand Prix driver Mika Hakkinen?
      Finnish

60   Which team did Barcelona beat in the 1992 European Cup Final at Wembley?
      Sampdoria

61   Who won Olympic gold medals in the 110 metres hurdles in LA and Seoul?
      Roger Kingdom

62   Against which county did Brian Lara score his record 501 not out?
      Durham

63   Graeme Souness joined Middlesborough as a player from which club?
      Tottenham

64   With which sport do you associate Jacky Ickx?
      Motor Racing

65   Walker Smith was the real name of which world boxing legend?
      Sugar Ray Robinson

66   Clive Rice used to captain which county cricket team?
      Nottinghamshire

67   Which international superstar was, in 1997, reportedly offered £50,000 a week plus a helicopter to play for Everton?
      Jürgen Klinsmann

68   Who announced in 1996 that he would like to play for England in the 1998 World Cup at the age of 36?
      Stuart Pearce

69   Which county play their home matches at Edgbaston?
     Warwickshire

70   On which horse did Bob Champion win the Grand National in 1981?
     Aldaniti

71   How many times was Billy Wright capped by England?
     105

72   True or False? The USA team won Olympic gold at Rugby Union?
     True

73   Who was the first black England football international?
     Viv Anderson

74   What was the title of Scotland's 1982 World Cup hit song?
     'We Have a Dream'

75   Who made a record 72 international appearances for Ireland between 1974 and 1990 but never played in a World Cup?
     Liam Brady

76   In which sport is Alberto Tomba a legend?
     Skiing

77   Who was top goal-scorer in the 1986 World Cup?
     Gary Lineker

78   On which racecourse is the St Leger run?
     Doncaster

79   In which track event did David Hemery win an Olympic gold medal?
     400 metre Hurdles

80   Which was one major championship that eluded golfer Sam Snead?
     US Open

81   In which event was John Walker an Olympic champion?
     1500 metres

82   In which sport is Irina Rodnina a legend?
     Ice Skating

83   Who won the men's 100 metres in the 1995 World Athletics Championships?
     Donovan Bailey

84   Which country hosted the 1958 football World Cup?
     Sweden

85   What nationality was double gold hero Alberto Juantorena?
     Cuban

86   On which horse did Harry Llewellyn clinch an equestrian gold medal for Britain?
     Foxhunter

87 Which late TV commentator coached Olympic champion Lynn Davies?
Ron Pickering

88 Which 1966 World Cup hero was a first-class Cricketer?
Geoff Hurst

89 Which England captain shook Maradona's hand before the start of the 1986 World Cup finals?
Peter Shilton

90 Which 1966 World Cup hero was nicknamed El Bandito?
Nobby Stiles

91 Which Australian swimmer won 3 women's 100m freestyle golds?
Dawn Fraser

92 In which year did London last stage the Olympics?
1948

93 Who partnered Michael Stich to win the men's doubles in the 1992 Olympic tennis finals?
Boris Becker

94 Which Dutchman was sacked in 1996 after coaching Barcelona for 8 years?
Johan Cruyff

95 Who, in 1982, became the youngest player in the history of the World Cup Finals?
Norman Whiteside

96 What 7 words preceded Kenneth Wolstenholme's famous '....... they think it's all over'?
There are some people on the pitch

97 Who rode Moonshell to victory in The Oaks in 1995?
Frankie Dettori

98 Who took over from Jack Charlton as Ireland's manager?
Mick McCarthy

99 On which ground did Jim Laker take his record 19 wickets against Australia in 1956?
Old Trafford

100 How many times was Bobby Moore capped by England?
108

101 When hit, which ball travels the fastest tennis, football, cricket or golf?
Tennis

SPOOF QUESTIONS

1. Which top footballer's (ex-Sheffield Wednesday, Manchester City) father was a silent movie star?
Imri Varadi, Ollie Varadi (Oliver Hardy)

2. Name three Manchester United players whose second name is that of a flower?
Viollet, Blanchflower, Macdougall

3. Two pairs are taken to the FA Cup Final at Wembley and only one pair are used. What are they?
Coloured Ribbons for the FA Cup

4. Which Manchester United player of the 1980s shared the same name as a German newspaper?
Gerry Daly

5. Which Wembley final from the 1980s was named after a Dutch player?
Sherpa Van Trophy

6. Which seven teams from the Football League and Premier League have a 'building' in their name?
Arsenal, Newcastle, Aston Villa, Crystal Palace, Barnsley, Millwall, Barnet

7. Sunderland did it in 1979, Villa did it in 1981, who did it in 1980?
Brooking, Trevor (name of Cup Final-winning goalscorer)

8. Which teams played in a semi-final at Old Trafford and both wore white?
Lancashire and Yorkshire

9. Who plays at Wembley every year and does not receive a medal?
The Band

10. Which team won the FA Cup and never scored a goal?
Everton – John Never scored the winner

11. Which four English league football teams end with the letter 'e'?
Rochdale, C Palace, P Argyle, Port Vale

12. Name four sports events where, to win, the competitor(s) travel backwards.
Swimming, High Jump, Rowing, Tug of War

13. Who scored a penalty bare-footed live on TV against Peter Shilton?
Tony the Tiger (TV advert)

14. Who scored 6 goals in an FA Cup tie and ended up on the losing side?
Denis Law, Man City v Luton (Game was abandoned, City lost the replay)

15. Which Mancheter United manager had the name of a bird?
Matt Busby

16. Which famous England international footballer of the 1960s and 1970s had sisters who recorded a number one record?
Jimmy Greaves, Freeda Greaves (Three Degrees)

Your Name ....   Table No ....

CLEVER QUESTIONS

1   Name three players who hold a World Cup-winning medal and went on to manage a team who play at St James Park.
    Jack Charlton, Ossie Ardiles, Alan Ball
    (St James Park, home of Exeter City)

2   How many golf balls are there on the moon?
    3

3   What is the lowest score that cannot be thrown with only one dart?
    23

4   What is Muhammed Ali's real name in full?
    Cassius Marcellus Clay III

5   In which city did Gary Sobers hit his famous six sixes?
    Swansea

6   How many hands has Big Ben?
    None – it's a bell

7   How many World Cup Finals did George Best play in?
    None

8   What did Kettering Town do in the mid-1970s that made the FA tell them not to do it again, but everybody does it now?
    Had advertising on shirts in a match

9   In cricket, if every batsman is out first ball, what is the number of the last batsman at the crease?
    Number 8

10 What colour is Mayfair on a Monopoly Board?
    Dark Blue

11 What Australian soprano gave her name to a pudding?
    Dame Nellie Melba

12 How many legs has a Bombay Duck?
    None (it's a fish)

13 What is the name of Postman Pat's cat?
    Jess

14 Which footballer was transferred for £99,999.99 to avoid the pressure of becoming the first £100,000 player?
    Jimmy Greaves

Your Name ....   **Table No** ....

GUESS THE FACE

1
2
3
4
5
6
7
8
9
10
11
12
13
14
15
16

THE LOGO QUIZ

1

2

3

4

5

6

7

8

9

10

11

12

13

14

15

16

17

18

19

20

Guess the Face Quiz Answers

1	Calvin Klein
2	Prince William
3	Stuart Pearce
4	Lionel Blair
5	Pierce Brosnan
6	Madonna
7	Jesper Parnevic
8	Jim Carey
9	Paul Gambaccini
10	Shakin' Stevens
11	Paula Yates
12	Clarke Gable (Rhett Butler)
13	Ralph Lauren
14	Kristin Scott Thomas
15	Jack Nicholson
16	Richard Dreyfuss

The Logo Quiz Answers

1	The English Sports Council
2	The Royal Bank of Scotland
3	Mirror Group Newspapers
4	BT
5	Puma
6	Renault
7	Peugeot
8	The Football League
9	Reebok
10	Rotary International
11	Neff
12	Umbro
13	Kappa
14	Hewlett Packard
15	Vauxhall
16	Diadora
17	Adidas
18	Omega
19	Investors in People
20	Yellow Pages

Appendix II: Choosing an Agent

Picture the scene, the Local Football Club committee meeting. The subject, 'Who shall we get to speak at the annual dinner?' A bloke at the pub knows a friend of United's Striker and is sure he will do it for nothing. Sound familiar? If it comes off (chances of success 1%) the United Star Striker will not be an After Dinner Speaker and will have come along thinking he is to present the prizes. Result, embarrassment all round and probably the end of the Annual Dinner.

The scene changes to the Cricket Club with the subject similar, the Annual Fund Raising Sporting Dinner. The organiser has a brilliant idea. Ian Botham is sure to make the event a sell out and David Lloyd is a great speaker. 'Couldn't agree more,' say the Committee, 'what about the budget?' 'Ah yes, a grand should sort them out.' EACH! 'No way,' say the committee, '£500 each plus expenses, after all it is a cricket club dinner.' Weeks later the posters go up promoting the dinner with a former league umpire and 'Charlie Cheesey' the local comedian. Result, event cancelled.

For every horror story there are plenty of great successes. However, if you are in doubt seek help and advice.

Should we use an agent?

Much maligned, never trusted. But always remember an agent has a duty to get the best fee and terms of employment for his client. Fees are sometimes negotiable. It will depend on diary, travel and the desire of the sports personality or entertainer to want to support a function, or indeed their need to work.

An agent will contract you and a contract can work both ways. Remember, if you cancel then you will be required to pay all or a percentage of the fee lost. Should the personality have to drop out, an agent will usually work very hard to replace the personality with a similar speaker – often at very short notice. Indeed when a Speaker dropped out of a luncheon hours before the event in, of all places, **Cleethorpes, former Manchester United Manager, Wilf McGuinness,** got there not only in time to have a pre-dinner drink, but also went on to speak **brilliantly.**

Should we go direct?

Some Speakers like to deal **direct, but fee negotiation can become** embarrassing on occasions. When a speaker is new and hungry he will often give out his telephone number or card. **As he becomes more popular** and in greater demand, he will **usually work with a band of Speaker** Booking Agencies or Agents.

Who should we choose?

This is very much a budget consideration. An agency will be very happy to furnish you with a list of speakers and a general guide to fees and advice on important considerations such **as VAT and expenses. Always clarify** what the terms and conditions are. **For instance, you seek a speaker for a** fee of £1000. Then the invoice **arrives:**

Fee	£1000.00
Rail Travel, 1st Class	£155.00
Taxis	£45.00
Hotel	£100.00
	£1300.00
VAT	£227.50
TOTAL	£1527.50

Check every time what the fee **includes.**

It would be impossible in a book **to name every speaker or personality, and** those listed in Appendix III are **there to act as a rough guide and to give** you a few ideas. Not all of the **personalities listed will speak, but a non-**speaker could be an important **Guest of Honour or may do a question-and-**answer session.

Appendix III: Speakers and Comperes

The following lists are not intended to provide a full summary of all Speakers, Entertainers, Comedians, etc. In addition to these names there are hundreds more. Hopefully these lists will provide a useful sample of the After Dinner Entertainers who are available.

FOOTBALL

Alan Ball
Gordon Banks
Dave Bassett
George Best
Craig Brown
Steve Bruce
Terry Butcher
Sir Bobby Charlton
Jack Charlton
Ray Clemence
George Cohen
Jim Craig
Paddy Crerand
Tommy Docherty
Fred Eyre
Sir Tom Finney
Paul Fletcher
Tommy Gemmell
Johnny Giles
Jimmy Greaves
John Greig
Bruce Grobbelaar
Alan Hansen
Emlyn Hughes
Roger Hunt
Norman Hunter
Sir Geoff Hurst
Pat Jennings
Kevin Keegan

Alan Kennedy
Steve Kindon
Denis Law
Jim Leishman
John Lloyd
Sir Stanley Matthews
David Mellor
Wilf McGuinness
Duncan McKenzie
Alex McLeish
Frank McLintock
Lawrie McMenemy
Billy McNeill
George McNeill
Alan Mullery
Garry Nelson
David O'Leary
Peter Osgood
Martin Peters
David Pleat
Peter Shilton
Gordon Smith
Tommy Smith
Alan Stevenson
Nobby Stiles
Ian St John
Mike Summerbee
Graham Taylor
Norman Whiteside
Frank Worthington
Ron Yeats

RUGBY

Rob Andrew
Martin Bayfield
Bill Beaumont
Phil Bennett
Kyran Bracken
Gordon Brown
Peter Brown
Finlay Calder
Will Carling
Gareth Chilcott
Ben Clarke
Fran Cotton
Jonathan Davies
Mervyn Davies
John Dawes
David Duckham
Gareth Edwards
Jeremy Guscott
Gavin Hastings
John Jeffrey
Martin Johnson
Willie John McBride
Ian McGeechan
Bill McLaren
Kenny Milne
Brian Moore
Cliff Morgan
Dewi Morris
François Pienaar
Graham Price
Dean Richards
Ian Robertson
Mickey Skinner
Fergus Slattery
Steve Smith
David Sole
Roger Uttley
Rob Wainwright
Peter Wheeler

CRICKET

Jonathan Agnew
Paul Allott
Dennis Amiss
Michael Atherton
Dickie Bird
Henry Blofeld
Ian Botham
Geoffrey Boycott
Chris Broad
Mike Cowan
Chris Cowdrey
Lord Colin Cowdrey
Basil D'Oliveira
Ray East
Frances Edmonds
Godfrey Evans
Graeme Fowler
Graham Gooch
David Gower
Tom Graveney
Sir Richard Hadlee
Rachel Heyhoe-Flint
Allan Lamb
Tony Lewis
Dennis Lillee
David Lloyd
Graham Lloyd
Christopher Martin-Jenkins
Geoff Miller
Don Mosey
Mark Nicholas
Peter Parfitt
Dermot Reeve
Jack Simmons
Brian Statham
Jeff Thomson
Fred Trueman
Peter Walker
Mike Watkinson

OTHER SPORTS

Peter Alliss
Eric Bristow
Frank Bruno
Bob Champion
John Conteh
Henry Cooper
Steve Davis
Peter Fox
John Francome
Ray French
Bernard Gallacher
Reg Gutteridge
David Howes
Alex Hay
John McCrirrick
Barry McGuigan
Alan Minter
Adrian Moorhouse
Alex Murphy
Lord John Oaksey
Mary Peters
Richard Pitman
Ray Reardon
John Stirling
John H Stracey
Dennis Taylor
Billy Thompson
Jim Watt

SPECIALIST SPEAKERS

Graham Davies
Derek Hatton
Peter Brown
Eric Jones
Dr Kevin Jones
David Kendall
Peter Maloney

Brian Voile Morgan
Cynthia Payne
Judge Pickles
Barry Roberts
John Stalker
Stan Taylor
David Gunson
Barry Williams

PERSONALITIES/ENTERTAINERS

Phil Cool
Max Boyce
Peter Brackley
Kevin Connelly
Roger De Courcey
Rory Bremner
Dougie Donnelly
Hazel Irvine
Michael Parkinson
Garry Richardson
Robbie Glen
Mike Osman
Bob 'the Cat' Bevan
George Duffus
John McGee
Rex Warner
Andy Cameron
Craigie Veitch
Dave Hill
Alisair McGowan

COMPERES

Dave Buck
Ken Davies
Mick Docherty
David Duckham
David Howes

Dave Jones
Mark Jones
Malcolm Lord
Neil Midgley
Vince Miller
James Reeve
Norman Vernon
Elton Welsby

Seth Sheldon
Gary Skyner
Sean Styles
Syd Tate
Venn Tracy
Trevor Wallace
Malcolm J White
Dave Wolfe
Dusty Young

COMEDIANS

Billy Bean
Paul Boardman
Stan Boardman
Jimmy Bright
Jim Bowen
Frank Carson
Johnny Casson
Eddie Colinton
Ivor Davies
Mike Farrell
Mickey Finn
Tony Gerrard
Paddy Green
Mickey Gunn
Charlie Hale
Johnny Hammond
Aaron James
Franklin James
Trevor James
Tony Jo
Mike Kelly
Mike King
Austin Knight
Mike Lancaster
Bernard Manning
Willie Miller
Tom O'Connor
Tom Pepper
George Roper
Abi Senior

Looking to the future

If you have found the information in this book helpful and would like to receive updated information on speakers, comperes etc., plus any new fund-raising ideas, please complete the form below. We will add your information to our marketing database and keep you posted of anything we feel may be of interest to you.

Name: . . . .   **Position:** . . . .

Organisation: . . . .   **Sport:** . . . .

Address: . . . .

. . . .

. . . .   **Postcode:** . . . .

Telephone: . . . .   **Fax:** . . . .

E-mail: . . . .

Please forward to:

The Dinner Business
MBN Promotions
Builder House
2 Mayors Road
ALTRINCHAM
Cheshire WA15 9RP

We suggest you photocopy this page, rather than tearing it out of the book.

NOTES AND OTHER IDEAS

NOTES AND OTHER IDEAS

NOTES AND OTHER IDEAS

NOTES AND OTHER IDEAS

NOTES AND OTHER IDEAS

NOTES AND OTHER IDEAS

NOTES AND OTHER IDEAS